NEW DIRECTIONS IN MORAL

Geoffrey Chapman Pastoral Studies Series

Making RCIA work, handling the management of change and loss, parish evangelization, diocesan renewal, moral theology at the end of the twentieth century, the challenges raised by *Christifideles Laici*, reconciliation, these are all issues to be covered in the Geoffrey Chapman Pastoral Studies series.

For the clergy, pastoral workers and interested lay people, the series is based on experience, and provides a comprehensive introduction to the issues involved.

The authors are recognized authorities on their subjects and bring their considerable experience and expertise to bear on the series.

NEW DIRECTIONS IN MORAL THEOLOGY

The Challenge of Being Human

KEVIN T. KELLY

GEOFFREY
CHAPMAN

Geoffrey Chapman
An imprint of Cassell Publishers Limited
Villiers House, 41/47 Strand, London WC2N 5JE, England
387 Park Avenue South, New York, NY 10016-8810, USA

First published 1992

British Library Cataloguing-in-Publication Data
A catalogue record for this book is available from the British Library.

Library of Congress Cataloging-in-Publication Data
Kelly, Kevin T., 1933–
    New directions in moral theology: the challenge of being human/
    Kevin T. Kelly.
      p.   cm. — (Geoffrey Chapman pastoral studies series)
    Includes index.
    ISBN 0-225-66639-1
    1. Christian ethics—Catholic authors.   2. Man (Christian
theology) I. Title. II. Series.
    BJ1249.K42   1992
    241'042—dc20   91-37198
                                                               CIP

ISBN 0-225-66639-1

Typeset by Colset Private Limited, Singapore
Printed and bound in Great Britain by
Biddles Ltd, Guildford and King's Lynn

CONTENTS

PREFACE

When I was in the process of writing an earlier book on divorce and second marriage, a friend of mine asked me what kind of reader I was writing for. I found that a difficult question to answer. In the end I replied that I was probably writing the book for myself. I felt that if I could get my own thinking clearer on that difficult and complex theological and pastoral issue, that might be of some help to others too. I suppose I would say the same thing if I was asked who I was writing this book for. When the publisher approached me about it, I was very hesitant at first. In the end I agreed to have an attempt at it. I thought that it might force me to clarify my own thinking on a number of topics which I have discussed with my students without committing myself to one side or the other in the debate.

I do not claim to be an original thinker, nor a deep thinker. I am a run-of-the-mill teacher of moral theology who has read fairly widely in the field and who has tried to listen a lot. I am convinced that moral theology at the present time is facing questions of immense importance at the level of both methodology and practice. Most of this book deals with the first of these two levels but I believe that the questions involved have far-reaching practical implications.

My thinking is not original but I hope it is personal. I have tried to listen carefully to the thinking of other people but that does not mean I have listened uncritically. In other words, I have tried to evaluate this thinking and look at its implications for practical moral living. My own personal situation is helpful to this process. As well as lecturing in Christian ethics at Heythrop College in the University of London, I am also charged with pastoral responsibility for the parish of Our Lady's, Eldon Street, in the northern sector of inner-city Liverpool. There is no doubt in my mind that the people in whose midst I am privileged to live in Liverpool play an important role in my understanding of Christian ethics. The very down-to-earth love and wisdom that is evident in their everyday living, despite all its hardship and ambiguity, provides an important resource for Christian ethics. I am fortunate in being able to draw on their expertise, crafted in the school of experience over many generations. Moreover, what bearing, if any, a topic discussed in Christian ethics has on their lives provides me with a touchstone for testing out how important such a topic might be for real life. Someone writing about life in the city of Liverpool recently spoke of it as a 'universe-city'. I honestly believe that this book owes at least as much to my belonging to the universe-city of Liverpool as it does to my involvement in the University of London.

Obviously, writing a book like this involves being open to self-criticism when some of the thinking in it touches on some fundamental moral questions about which there is evidence of deep concern in the Church. A good friend of mine once remarked that he would love to hear a Pastoral Letter beginning with the words 'I may be wrong but—'. In a sense, I would like the reader to imagine those words written at the top of every page of this book. This is because I believe that truth statements on some highly debated issues in the field of morality are difficult to arrive at and hence any attempt to articulate them must be presented with due modesty and must lay itself open to critical questions. Moreover, these truth statements have a certain note of provisionality about them. Insofar as they are true, they are a partial statement of the truth. They are certainly not the whole truth, nor are they necessarily the best expression of this partial grasp of the truth. But more of that later in the book.

Here and there in the book what I have written impinges on Roman Catholic moral teaching. I could have written a 'safe' book. If I had done so, I believe I would have been unfaithful to my 'ecclesial vocation' as a moral theologian. I believe strongly in my Church. It is this belief which gives me the confidence to say what I regard as the truth within the Catholic Church. I believe there is great wisdom and love in my Church. I recognize too that there is also unwisdom and unlove in my Church. To be afraid to voice what I think is true would be tantamount to saying that I believe that unwisdom and unlove is stronger than wisdom and love in my· Church. And that I do not believe. Moreover, I hope I am ready to recognize that there is a fair share of unwisdom and unlove in me. And since to a large extent that can be presumed to take the form of blindness, I am probably unaware of its operation in me and its influence on my thinking and writing. That is an added reason for the subliminal message 'I may be wrong but —' inscribed at the top of every page. If my unwisdom and unlove have led me to put forward some foolish or unloving moral positions in this book, I believe that there is enough wisdom and love in my Church to cope with that and set the record straight.

I have already called on some of that wisdom and love by showing parts of the drafts of my book to a number of fellow Christians whom I would regard as 'experts' either because of their professional competence or their experience at the coal-face of life in the raw. I also respect them for their wise and loving living and I know that their wisdom and love would lead them to point out to me any unwisdom and unlove in what I have written. In this connection I would like to thank particularly Dr Bernard Hoose, Professor Ellen Leonard, Dr Gerard J. Hughes and Dr Anne Murphy. I would never have been able to write this book without the encouragement and practical help given me by Fr Jim Dunne. Thanks to his hard work and dedication I knew that the people back home in Liverpool would not be neglected while I was busy on my word processor at Heythrop College. I must also thank Anne King from Geoffrey Chapman. She first talked me into writing this book and her gentle patience and understanding kept the project alive when the going was hard.

In the Nash Lecture for 1988 Richard McCormick offered his dream for moral theology in the year 2000 and expressed his hope that such a future moral theology would be both universal and ecumenical. In saying that, he is not ditching the specifically *Christian* dimension nor is he wanting to deny the existence of a *Catholic* tradition of moral theology. He is saying, however, that moral theology must have 'some persuasiveness in general experience' and hence must not be sectarian and outside the normal domain of public moral discourse. The purpose of this book is to explore some of the implications of such a moral theology.

Chapter 1
DIALOGUE AND DIVERSITY IN THE DECADE
OF EVANGELIZATION

Listening to the experience of wise and loving people

This book is as much about evangelization as it is about moral theology. That is because it is based on the belief that there is an intimate link between Christian morality and evangelization. Without denying the uniqueness and importance of Christian revelation, I believe that our most committed profession of faith in God is made not in words but in the way we live our lives. That is true equally of Christians and non-Christians. That is why the moral life is so important.

The moral life is not an invention of Judeo-Christian theologians. It is as old as the human family itself. It is about how human persons treat themselves and each other with respect. For respect to be real it needs to be translated into respectful behaviour. Yet deciding in a particular situation what is respectful behaviour is not always easy. Very often it can only be discovered by a wise and loving heart as it learns from experience, listening to other wise and loving hearts, and then making its own way as it lives its own unique and unrepeatable life and thus carves a new image of God, destined to live for eternity.

In the centuries following the Reformation up until Vatican II, Roman Catholics tended to see themselves as members of the 'only true Church'. Whatever seed of truth was contained in that statement was distorted by its being given an exclusivist interpretation. This was commonly taken to imply that only Roman Catholics (and principally those who were church-goers, of course) were in a 'state of grace' and so had wise and loving hearts. Added to this, Roman Catholics had also been inclined to assume that their religious leaders, especially the pope and the bishops, were endowed with special gifts of wisdom and love. Hence they drew their ideas about respectful living principally from this source. Authoritative teaching was given greater credence than what people had learnt from their own personal experience. And certainly no credence was given to the experience of those who were outside the Church.

Vatican II reversed this trend. It brought back into focus God's invitation to all people to share in his goodness and holiness. It helped Catholics to see their fellow Christians and their Churches through new and more appreciative eyes. It acknowledged the unique place of the Jews in God's saving plan and recognized the religious authenticity of non-Christian religions. It encouraged Catholics to see the Christian 'new creation' present and active in the lives of all people of good will and to believe that God's revelation and saving will is at work even outside Judaism and Christianity. Along with this switch from a negative to a positive focus went a renewed emphasis on the dignity of the human person and the importance of listening to life and learning from experience.

Obviously, human experience itself is as old as the human race itself. It is not a new discovery that only came into existence after Vatican II. A wise medieval monk once said: 'We see further than our forebears: we are like dwarfs sitting on the shoulders of giants'. As with the rest of the human family, down through the centuries the Roman Catholic Church has built up a vast experience of loving and wise living. Teaching authority has seen one of its roles as preserving this tradition for us and making it available for our upbuilding as wise and loving persons. It would be a foolish person who discarded such a treasure or who claimed it had nothing to offer us today.

However, there is a shadow side to tradition within the Roman Catholic Church as within the human family as a whole. As Karl Rahner has pointed out, although holiness is one of the marks of the Church, we are also a Church of sinners — and that means all of us, including popes and bishops. Hence, mixed in with the lived experience of wisdom and love in our tradition there is also much unwisdom and unlove. It was largely because he was keenly aware of this that Pope John XXIII felt the need to call the Second Vatican Council. His successor, Paul VI, in his opening address to the Second Session of the Council, showed his appreciation of this by stressing the reforming character of the Council:

> We have just spoken of the Bride of Christ looking upon Christ to discern in him her true likeness. If in doing so she were to discover some shadow, some defect, some stain upon her wedding garment, what should be her instinctive, courageous reaction? There can be no doubt that her primary duty would be to reform, correct and set herself aright in con-

formity with her divine model. (Yves Congar, Hans Küng and Daniel O'Hanlon (eds), *Council Speeches of Vatican II* (Sheed & Ward, 1964), p. 51)

John Paul II uses a similar image when he insists that this self-reforming exercise must be an ongoing process if the Church and individual Christians are to proclaim the Gospel by the witness of their lives. This demands 'a personal and communal examination of conscience in order to correct in their behaviour whatever is contrary to the Gospel and disfigures the face of Christ' (*Redemptoris Missio*, n. 44).

One result of this ongoing renewal in the Roman Catholic Church is that the experience of wise and loving non-Catholic Christians, non-Christians and all women and men of good will is now seen as a rich Spirit-inspired source on which the Church can draw in trying to understand what form respectful living should take in our own day and age.

Dialogue and the renewal of moral theology

Vatican II committed the Roman Catholic Church to emerge from its ghetto. The Pastoral Constitution on The Church in the World of Today was a prime example of this renewal. It virtually takes the form of a dialogue with the contemporary world, listening to and sharing in 'its hopes and joys, its sufferings and anxieties', as its very title, *Gaudium et Spes*, suggests. It attempts to listen to the movement of God's Spirit in the heart of the human family and through this listening tries to discern 'the signs of the times'. Moreover, it calls for dialogue with all men and women of good will. This dialogue is to be inclusive, embracing men and women of all faiths and even those who are professedly atheist. It is this Vatican II emphasis on dialogue which has inspired the basic thrust of this book.

Struggling to live a fully human life is the principal way in which the members of the human family profess their faith in God, whether they are aware of it or not. Hence, if we as members of that family are to come to understand what kind of moral living is most pleasing to God at this point in history, we must draw on all the riches of wise and loving human experience that are available to us. John Paul II expresses this very vividly in his 1990 encyclical letter *Redemptoris Missio*, when he states: '[Dialogue] is demanded by deep respect for everything that has been brought about in human beings by the

Spirit who blows where he wills' (n. 56). This means that we must really listen to each other, trying to appreciate what values in life make each of us tick. That is not just a matter of listening to individuals. It also means listening to other communities, organizations or movements of committed people whose value systems may not be exactly the same as our own or who may order their priorities differently to ourselves.

In plumping for dialogue on such a wide scale Vatican II was implicitly admitting that in no way does the Roman Catholic Church have all the answers. It was recognizing that Christian revelation involves a continuing common search as well as a privileged tradition. In fact, that privileged tradition would not be properly preserved and respected if this continuing common search was neglected or abandoned. In this Vatican II approach to the world even infallibility need not be seen as a conversation-stopper but merely as putting down a clear marker as we struggle forward on our journey of discovery.

The belief in moral dialogue with flows from Vatican II is based on a historically and culturally conscious approach to moral knowledge. It is to accept that human experience is an indispensable and fundamental source for our moral knowledge. Cardinal Hume more than hinted at this in his magnificent intervention at the 1983 Rome Synod on the Family (cf. p. 66 below). Through our experience we come to discover ways of living which really are wise and loving and we also learn how to distinguish these forms of behaviour from those which are unwise and unloving. However, the moral knowledge thus acquired, though true, is only partial. It still remains historically and culturally conditioned. Hence, it might not be an adequate guide for wise and loving living in another culture or at a different period in history. Nor does it exclude the possibility that there might be alternative ways of behaving which might be equally wise and loving.

However, as a precondition for moral dialogue, Vatican II presumes that there are certain basic values that are common to the whole human family and which flow from our common humanity. Theologically, the Council could be interpreted as saying that at this level we are on holy ground. Respect for these values has an element of reverence about it since here we are dealing with the image of God in each of us.

It is precisely because we share this basic humanity that we are able to dialogue in our diversity. It is our common humanity which enables us to appreciate the richness of our diversity. Dialogue, in fact, is the expression of this appreciation and involves a positive approach to the phenomenon of disagreement on moral issues. It can even be open to the possibility that basic human values can be lived out in radically different ways and can give rise to a plurality of moral stances. Dialogue with those who differ from us is an essential element in the way the methodology of moral theology is understood today. Nevertheless, in no way does this imply that contemporary moral theology subscribes to moral relativism, or denies the existence of any kind of objective moral truth or reduces morality to the level of personal preference.

Dialogue is also a prerequisite for evangelization. As Paul VI put it so forcefully, evangelization is not simply about enabling others to hear the good news. It is equally about hearing the good news ourselves:

> The church is an evangelizer, but she begins by being evangelized herself . . . She needs to listen unceasingly to what she must believe . . . She has a constant need of being evangelized, if she wishes to retain freshness, vigour and strength in order to proclaim the Gospel . . . The church . . . is evangelized by constant conversion and renewal, in order to evangelize the world with credibility. (*Evangelii Nuntiandi*, n. 15)

John Paul II makes the same point even more briefly: 'We cannot preach conversion unless we ourselves are converted anew every day' (*Redemptoris Missio*, n. 47). In dialogue we are involved in the evangelization process — sharing with others the good news as we understand it and in turn listening to others sharing with us the good news as they understand it.

Belief in dialogue also has implications for moral teaching. Although a moral teacher may enjoy personal authority, due to his or her own wisdom or learning, nevertheless he or she is still teaching as a member of a wider learning community and so even his or her most authoritative teaching is still far from being the whole truth and can at most only be seen as the best expression of the truth as he or she understands it for the present. This obviously has important implications for those who exercise the office of moral teachers, especially the pope, the Roman Curia and the bishops. Because their teaching authority is not based on their *personal* authority but on their *official* role in the learning community of the Church, it is a prerequisite for the responsible exercise of this office that the richest moral understanding in the community is listened to. Even when it is, this exercise of teaching authority is still subject to the same limitations as mentioned previously. It should be presented as the best way they can express the truth for the present. If official Church teachers exercise their office in this way, they have the right to expect those they serve to give their teaching what Richard McCormick calls 'the presumption of the truth'. If they neglect this dialogue process or unduly limit its scope, they do a disservice to the credibility of their office and thereby forfeit the presumption of the truth for their teaching.

Celebrating life and living the truth

The evangelizing mission of the Church is not to stand up in society and condemn the values according to which people are living their lives. Such a stance might have the superficial attraction of seeming to be 'counter-cultural' and so faithful to the prophetic mission of the Crucified One whose Gospel we proclaim. However, that is a false understanding of the counter-cultural character of the Gospel. To be counter-cultural should never be the *direct* aim of the Church. Such an approach would be reminiscent of the negative way in which the Gospel recipe for life has sometimes been presented. Hugh Lavery gently parodies this in his inimitable way: 'In the beginning was the Word, and the Word was NO!'

Before being counter-cultural, the Church must first be procultural. It must tune in carefully to the positive values according to which most people are trying to live good and committed lives. The Church must evangelize itself by listening to and learning from those values. In a sense, evangelization in any society is about first of all absorbing the positive values which motivate people in their lives; and then, secondly, having absorbed those values, it is about standing up and celebrating them and giving thanks (eucharist) for them. It is implicitly saying of these values, 'This is the Word of the Lord — for today'. This is the proper meaning of being 'pro-life'. This is how the Church should exercise its teaching authority in the area of morals. It should confirm people's faith by articulating and affirming the human values which are embodied in the lives of committed men and women, struggling to be true to that wisdom and love which we believe God has placed deep in their hearts.

The counter-cultural dimension comes in later. If the Church tries to give people confidence to believe in their own goodness and in the goodness of their fellow men and women, it is embarking on a confrontation course. If people can be helped to believe that the world really can be an even better place than it is, if people can be encouraged to have the confidence to believe that they themselves, other people and human institutions are capable of living an even fuller human life than they are doing at present, a lot of vested interests will very soon come to be threatened. It is then that the 'voice of original sin', as Sebastian Moore calls it, will be heard (cf. *Let This Mind Be in You* (Darton, Longman & Todd, 1985), chapters 24–26). That voice does not believe in our God-given dignity and responsibility. The voice of original sin refuses to accept the faith God has in us. 'Be realistic', it says, 'things cannot really be changed. Life will always be as it is. That is just human nature. We will never be any different. You might as well settle for the mediocre or second-best.' The Good News is that original sin is proclaiming an untruth. Original sin is urging us to live our lives according to a lie. The Gospel exposes that lie. 'The truth will make you free.'

One of the most powerful recent expositions of this is Václav Havel's brilliant essay *The Power of the Powerless*. He is discussing the case of a shopkeeper to whom a Communist Party official gives his regular Party poster to be displayed in his shop window. The shopkeeper knows that no one will actually read what is written on the poster, just as he himself will not read it. Nevertheless, by displaying the poster he plays his little part in maintaining the lie on which the whole system is built. He is living within that lie like everyone else. However, if the shopkeeper decides not to display the poster, the whole system is threatened. That is because by refusing to live within the lie he touches a raw nerve in everyone else. That nerve is the openness to truth that lies deep within everyone living the lie. His action, therefore, really is subversive. Building on this example he goes on to present, in completely non-theological language, what Sebastian Moore would prefer to call the untruth of original sin:

> The essential aims of life are present naturally in every person. In everyone there is some longing for humanity's rightful dignity, for moral integrity, for free expression of being and a sense of transcendence over the world of existence. Yet, at the same time, each person is capable, to a greater or lesser degree, of coming to terms with living within the lie. Each person somehow succumbs to a profane trivialization of his or her inherent humanity, and to utilitarianism. In everyone there is some

willingness to merge with the anonymous crowd and to flow comfortably along with it down the river of pseudo-life . . .

Individuals can be alienated from themselves only because there is something in them to alienate. The terrain of this violation is their authentic existence. Living the truth is thus woven directly into the texture of living a lie. It is the repressed alternative, the authentic aim to which living a lie is an inauthentic response . . . Under the orderly surface of the life of lies, therefore, there slumbers the hidden sphere of life in its real aims, of its hidden openness to truth. (*Living in Truth* (Faber & Faber, 1989), pp. 54, 57)

In Chapter 3, I shall try to explore these 'essential aims of life' which Havel believes are naturally present in every person. However, prior to that it might be instructive to look at a contemporary example of disagreement both between Christians and also between other committed men and women in our society.

Disagreement between Christian Churches

The day the House of Commons began debating the Human Fertilization and Embryology Bill, *The Times* (23 April 1990) carried two items which presented readers with an extraordinary contrast of positions, made even more remarkable by the fact that they were on pages facing each other.

The first was a joint letter from the five Roman Catholic Archbishops of England and Wales (Cardinal Hume and Archbishops Worlock of Liverpool, Bowen of Southwark, Couve de Murville of Birmingham and Ward of Cardiff). It called for a clear rejection of destructive experimentation on embryos on the grounds that 'from the beginning of the fertilization process the embryo is new human life' and 'this fact alone should govern its status, dignity and rights under the law'. They asserted that 'justice requires that an equality of respect be given to all human life as such, and not merely in virtue of its characteristics, attributes or achievement' and claimed that 'it is precisely this principle with underpins the protection which should be extended by the law to all'.

They concluded: 'If the moral principle of respect for human life is reduced to the level of a subjective preference, we further erode the foundations of our British system of justice'. How deeply these convictions go was further evidenced by a very strong statement by Cardinal Hume speaking on behalf of his fellow bishops. The statement followed the Commons vote in favour of permitting embryo experimentation during the first fourteen days. Part of it reads as follows:

> The importance which I and my fellow bishops attach to these developments in relation to embryo experimentation and abortion cannot be overstressed. What has emerged with stark clarity is the lack of a moral foundation for the formation of public policy in this most crucial area, that of human life and death.
>
> In fact as a society we have abandoned fundamental aspects of Christian morality. Specifically we have dispensed with the traditional Christian vision of the sanctity of human life. We can no longer claim to be a truly Christian society. (Full text in *Briefing* (4 May 1990), pp. 164–5)

The contrasting article on the opposite page of *The Times* was written by John Habgood, Archbishop of York. Archbishop Habgood had earlier, in the debate in the House of Lords on 7 December 1989, supported the Bill's clause favouring embryo research and had expressed the hope that 'we can come through this stage of sharp confrontation towards a consensus which acknowledges the special quality of human embryonic life but which refuses nevertheless to make claims to it which are biologically, theologically and philosophically unsustainable, and which recognises a valid place for research in this delicate area' (*Hansard* (7 December 1989), col. 1022). In his *Times* article, the Archbishop claimed that the embryo debate was not calling in question 'basic principles on which all people of good will might expect to agree', but it was getting into difficulties on the fundamental issue as to what kind of enlightenment we can expect from our Christian faith on such a question:

> The sanctity of human life, the need to give special protection to the weakest and most vulnerable, a consciousness of human limitations and of the dangers of arrogance and self-deception — all are moral starting points which to my mind are not in question. But I cannot accept the· claims that the Scriptures and Christian tradition give us authoritative moral and theological guidance about the precise point at which the complex processes entailed in the beginnings of an individual human life give it unique moral status.

He is careful to note that many Christian opponents of embryo research 'are careful not to make excessive claims, do admit large areas of uncertainty, and reach their conclusions on a balance of probabilities, with a general bias towards caution'. He then proceeds to present the arguments in favour of 'the morally significant dividing line' occurring either at fourteen days or at implantation and notes that 'moral arguments such as these rest on the interpretation of scientific evidence, and it should not be surprising if sincere and godly people disagree'. His own belief is 'that the balance of the argument is in favour of the 14-day rule' and hence he is prepared to argue that embryo research, under suitable safeguards, 'opens the way to a reverential sharing in the mystery of God's creativity, as well as the relief of human suffering'. He recognizes that he differs from some fellow Christians on this matter but queries whether this should be a cause of scandal and bewilderment. In fact, he opens his article on this very note:

> Why should Christians believe that their faith gives them unique and authoritative insights into problems which are substantially new? A moral response which allows tentative exploration of new possibilities, with many checks and balances, may be nearer the mind of God, who knows both our strengths and our weaknesses, than outright acceptance or rejection.

This striking contrast of Christian positions evokes memories of 1930 when the Lambeth Conference first began to query the long-standing Christian condemnation of contraception and opened the door slightly to its acceptance. This prompted Pius XI to issue his encyclical letter *Casti Connubii*, in which, 'gazing out upon the world from the watchtower of this Apostolic See', he raised 'Our voice in warning to the flock committed to Our care, to keep them away from poisoned pastures' (n. 3). And on the specific issue of contraception, he wrote: 'The Catholic church, to whom God has committed the task of teaching and preserving morals and right conduct in their integrity, standing erect amidst this moral devastation, raises her voice in sight of her divine mission to keep the chastity of the marriage contract unsullied by this ugly stain . . .'

Many Christians will be wondering what on earth is going on here. They would find it hard to believe that Pius XI is suggesting that the Anglican bishops are leading their flock into 'poisoned pastures' and that the Lambeth Conference is giving teaching which leads to 'moral devastation'! Likewise, they would find it equally hard to believe that the Roman Catholic bishops are implying that the Archbishop of York has 'abandoned fundamental aspects of Christian morality' and 'dispensed with the traditional Christian vision of the sanctity of human life'! Clearly it is important to look at the issues which are raised by this kind of fundamental disagreement between Christian Churches.

The kind of questions I am trying to wrestle with in this book are less personalized but perhaps even more important. They would include such questions as: Does disagreement on important moral issues imply mutual condemnation of the opposing position? Is diversity a scandal or could it be a valuable stage along the road towards better understanding? Does moral pluralism need to be interpreted as based on a moral system of subjective preference? When interpretations of empirical data have to be made in order to arrive at a moral evaluation of an issue, how are disagreements about differing interpretations to be handled? Does the Christian faith offer privileged insights on moral issues? What are we to make of the statement of the Second Vatican Council that 'In fidelity to conscience, Christians are joined with the rest of men [and women surely — *my addition*] in the search for truth, and for the genuine solution to the numerous problems which arise in the life of individuals from social relationships' (*Gaudium et Spes*, n. 16)? Does it mean that we are all engaged in a common search as members of God's human family and, as such, are we obliged to respect the integrity and scientific or philosophical competence of committed men and women who do not share our Christian faith?

Faced with such radical disagreement on the issue of embryo research it is interesting to note the different reactions of the Roman Catholic archbishops and Archbishop Habgood. Cardinal Hume and his fellow Roman Catholic archbishops appeal to the 'absolute' nature of fundamental moral criteria. They accuse the opposing position of 'abandoning fundamental aspects of Christian morality' and 'dispensing with the traditional Christian view of the sanctity of human life'. They even goes so far as to say that a nation which rejects the position they represent 'can no longer claim to be a truly Christian society'.

Archbishop Habgood, on the other hand, does not find it 'surprising if sincere and godly people disagree'. His own belief does not claim absolute certainty but is based on 'the balance of the argument'. He even suggests that 'a moral response which allows tentative exploration of new possibilities, with many checks and balances, may be nearer the mind of God, who knows both our strengths and our weaknesses, than outright acceptance or rejection'.

Many people were probably shocked by such a public disagreement between moral teachers. What price ecumenism and united witness when there seems to exist such radical disagreement between the leaders of the two main Christian Churches in the country!

There are two ways in which such an instance of disagreement between Christian moral teachers could be examined. The first would be to analyse in closer detail the issue of embryo research and see if the disagreement could be resolved or if perhaps it might not be as deep-rooted as might appear on the surface. That is the kind of approach I adopted in a previous book, *Life and Love: Towards a Christian Dialogue on Bioethical Questions* (Collins, 1987), which dealt with the allied topic of in-vitro fertilization. The second way would be to prescind from this particular instance of disagreement and examine the more general question of disagreement about issues of morality and its implications for Christian moral teaching and witness. It is this second approach that will be followed in this book.

Chapter 2

GRACEFUL DISAGREEMENT

Disagreement without mutual condemnation

We have seen that Christian Churches can disagree on moral issues
of major importance. Disagreement about the status of the embryo
immediately after conception is implicitly disagreement about
whether the life of the embryo is owed the same respect as the life
of any other human being. For those who agree with Archbishop
Habgood and hold that the early embryo is not owed such respect
there is no in-principle objection to embryo research, all other things
considered. For those who agree with the Roman Catholic archbishops and believe that such respect is owed to the early embryo,
the very thought of embryo experimentation is ethically repugnant.
Although both sides firmly believe in respect for human life based
on the God-given dignity of the human person, they disagree on
whether the early embryo is an instance in which that respect is
involved. Clearly, therefore, both sides would see this disagreement
as having major consequences with regard to ethical practice.

Nevertheless, neither side condemns the other as immoral.
Despite their fundamental disagreement they recognize each other's
good faith. In these ecumenical days we take this for granted. All the
same, its implications are worth closer examination. We need to
look at what is implied in the Roman Catholic archbishops' recognizing the good faith of Archbishop Habgood and vice versa.

Moral disagreement can sometimes be due to what is often
referred to as 'moral blindness'. This usually takes the form of a
more or less deliberate refusal to acknowledge the truth because the
consequences of this would be too disturbing. It might mean rocking
the boat or threatening one's own and others' vested interests. For
instance, in responding to apartheid the Christian Churches did not
say that they disagreed with it but acknowledged the good faith of
the South African regime. They said it was immoral and condemned
the moral blindness of its supporters. I take it that neither the Roman
Catholic archbishops nor Archbishop Habgood, despite their profound disagreement, would want to accuse each other of moral
blindness.

Sometimes moral disagreement comes about because of an ignorance on the part of one or other person which is best described as
crass or supine ignorance. This kind of ignorance means that a person has stupidly or stubbornly failed to take the easily available
appropriate means to dispel his or her ignorance. Once again I am
sure that neither the Catholic archbishops nor Archbishop Habgood
would want to accuse the other of such ignorance.

What is common to both moral blindness and crass or supine
ignorance is that both can easily be rectified. Moreover, since bad
will is at least implicit in each of these categories, they would be
classified as 'culpably vincible ignorance'.

It would be unthinkable to ascribe the disagreement between
Roman Catholic archbishops and Archbishop Habgood as being
due to the 'culpably vincible ignorance' of either of them. It is on a
totaly different plane. Both recognize the other's good faith.
Presumably that means that they do not regard the other's unacceptable view as detracting from their personal goodness. Would it be
fair to imagine Cardinal Hume (speaking for his fellow bishops) and
Archbishop Habgood saying to each other:

> I recognize your personal goodness and integrity. I also recognize that
> you must be convinced of the reasons on which your position is based.
> Although I do not find these reasons compelling myself, I cannot deny
> that you are an honest and intelligent person and so there must be some-
> thing in these reasons if they appeal to you so strongly. I also recognize
> that you are a good Christian and so you must find the position you hold
> to be in conformity with your Christian faith. Moreover, as a Christian
> leader convinced of the truth of your position, you are prepared to put it
> forward both as a guide for practical action and even as worthy of con-
> sideration by those who have the duty of determining public policy.
> Nevertheless, despite all that, I disagree profoundly with you. Quite
> frankly I think your view is wrong.

It would seem, therefore, that experience teaches us that it is
possible to have deep disagreement on a matter of major ethical
importance without the parties to the disagreement feeling they
must condemn each other ethically. The Roman Catholic bishops
believe that ethically embryo experimentation involves a major
violation of human dignity. Yet presumably they would not want to
accuse Archbishop Habgood of the sin of 'scandal', even though in
their eyes the Archbishop is implicitly encouraging people to do what
is ethically wrong. How can moral theology make any sense of this
kind of disagreement? I would suggest that it might help if we began

by looking at how the terms 'good/bad' and 'right/wrong' are used in moral theology.

Determining the rightness or wrongness of actions

Rightness and wrongness are categories which apply to human actions. To say an action is right or wrong does not *in itself* say anything about the goodness or badness of the person doing that action. It is simply saying that this action is not conducive to the human well-being or fulfilment of myself or others or the good of the rest of creation.

However, to speak of rightness and wrongness in this way, though not incorrect, is an over-simplification. It can give the impression that there is a total separation between the action and the person performing the action. Obviously, there is no human action without a human person performing it. That person not only 'performs' the action but also 'informs' it. In other words, he or she puts something of him- or herself into this action. It is impossible to give a true description of the 'meaning' of this particular action without taking account of the person performing it.

In considering the meaning of action it needs to be noticed that actions can come under a variety of general descriptions. The life-saving operation performed by Dr Jones can be described as 'moving a hand', 'lifting a knife', 'mutilating a limb', 'causing pain' and 'conducting a life-saving amputation'. While all those descriptions may be correct, they are not all equally relevant from the point of view of human meaningfulness. Obviously, 'mutilating a limb' and 'causing pain' are humanly significant. If these were the only humanly significant features of this action, then it would surely be judged to be detrimental to human well-being. To cause pain to a person or to cut off a person's limb are not exactly human goods. However, there is more to Dr Jones's action than that. It can also be described as a 'life-saving amputation'. The human physical evils of pain and mutilation are still dimensions of this action. They could be described as unavoidable negative features of the action which are compensated for by the greater good of the person's life being saved through this operation.

It is only when all the humanly significant descriptions of any particular action are seen in their totality that we are able to arrive at an adequate evaluation of the action. Prior to this point the partial descriptions of the action are merely saying that to the extent that a person's action fits into this or that category, to that extent the action will have within it this particular element which is conducive or detrimental to a certain aspect of human well-being. They are saying no more than this.

However, when an individual person faces the decision as to what is the best thing to do in a concrete situation, far more information might be needed than the fact that the action being contemplated can be categorized according to this or that partial description. There might be other partial descriptions of it as an action and these might alter the overall human significance of the action considered in its totality. In the instance we have been considering, the human-mutilating and pain-inflicting action of cutting off this person's leg has a human meaning other than mutilation and pain-infliction. It is also a 'life-saving' operation through amputating a possible source of infection for the rest of the body. In the case we are dealing with, this is its most humanly significant (its most important) meaning as a human action. To arrive at this most humanly significant meaning has necessarily involved us in some kind of human interpretation of the action. This interpretation has enabled us to grasp the *real* meaning of the action in this particular situation. Clearly, this process of interpreting the real meaning of this action (its significance as a whole) has involved us in an act of human judgement. Of course, whether we have judged rightly in our interpretation of this action is sometimes something we only learn from experience.

Experience enables us to refine much more clearly our moral categories. In the light of human experience much more complex and inclusive action-descriptions are formulated in an attempt to include the various factors of major human significance which are found together in certain ways of acting. This is how we come to develop our principles of moral evaluation. Such refinement tends to take place through the process of excluding kinds of actions which it is well-nigh impossible to imagine as being conducive to human well-being in any conceivable circumstances. These are the actions which we would refer to as being 'wrong in themselves' or 'intrinsically evil'. I have elaborated this point to bring out the fact that the link between the goodness or wickedness of a person and the rightness or wrongness of his or her action is far from simple.

Is morality about persons or action?

Moral theologians make a key distinction between 'goodness' (with its opposite, 'badness' or 'sinfulness') and 'rightness' (with its opposite 'wrongness'). Morality in the full and true sense of the word is about the goodness and badness of *persons* rather than about the rightness and wrongness of *actions*.

Only persons can be 'moral' in the proper sense of the word. The application of the term to describe human actions as such is derivative. 'Goodness' and 'badness' are terms descriptive of the moral state of a person. That moral state is determined by two factors. One is what the Bible would call the person's 'heart' — in other words, a person's basic stance in the face of life. Some modern writers refer to this as a person's 'fundamental option'. The other is the way a person lives his or her life as an individual, in relation to other individuals, and as a social being who is also part of the wider cosmos. This is the level on which a person works out the story of his or her life and in so doing becomes the person he or she is progressively choosing to be.

Clearly these two dimensions of a person's life are not two separate compartments. They are intrinsically interlinked and interactive. My heart registers the basic direction in which I live my life, while, conversely, individual choices and decisions are the very life-blood of my heart and at times may even provide the occasion for a change of heart, as in key moments of conversion or personal corruption.

Put very simply, personal goodness lies in setting one's heart on whatever one believes will best promote the well-being and fulfilment of oneself, other people and the rest of God's creation. Personal badness involves setting one's heart on a lesser or more partial good. In some way or other, this will take the form of making my own well-being and fulfilment the overriding consideration in my life and taking on board the well-being of others and the rest of creation only to the extent that I see this as serving my own well-being. This is not only a serious heart condition; it is also a form of blindness, since it fails to recognize that my own well-being as a human person is intrinsically bound up with being a person-for-others, an interpersonal being. In a sense, all sin comes down to a kind of 'reality evasion'.

Although there is some truth in saying that we become bad persons by doing wrong actions, that is a massive over-simplification. That is because we are the authors of our own actions. We cannot understand their meaning precisely as human actions if we do not take account of the meaning we ourselves infuse into the actions we perform. In this sense actions are like language. Language does not tell us what we should say. Language is the medium which enables us to express what we mean. Admittedly, we can misuse language. We may be mistaken about the precise meaning of certain words or expressions and may cause havoc or even offence and serious embarrassment as a result. At times we may say things we do not really mean. And on occasion we may use language to deceive others and hide our true meaning. What we cannot do is create our own private language. We cannot use words to mean just what we like. As a general rule, we have to abide by the meaning of words and the rules of grammar and syntax.

Applying this analogy to the rightness or wrongness of actions, it becomes clear that while kinds of actions (categorized *abstractly* according to certain general descriptions) may be recognized as having an intrinsic meaning just as words and sentences do, the meaning of actions *in the concrete* cannot be truly ascertained without looking at the meaning of this action as understood and intended by the person performing it.

The above analysis can throw some light on how the Roman Catholic archbishops and Archbishop Habgood can disagree radically, as they do, on the issue of embryo experimentation without either feeling obliged to condemn the other as morally bad. This is because, as we have seen, moral goodness or badness, insofar as it is related to particular actions, depends on how we interpret the meaning of the actions in question. In the case of Cardinal Hume, speaking for his fellow bishops, and Archbishop Habgood, each recognizes that the other is in good faith, while believing him to be in error. In this acknowledgement of good faith they would implicitly be saying to each other: 'I accept the integrity of your fundamental stance before life and I recognize that it is not compromised by your position on embryo experimentation since you interpret this action quite differently from the way I do'.

Acknowledging that the person is in good faith even though we believe that he or she is in error is one scenario for disagreement on moral issues. No doubt all of us have felt that to be the case in certain disagreements in which we ourselves have been involved. However, there is another and quite different way in which people can differ on matters of morality. This will become more evident if we turn our attention to the issue of what is sometimes called 'moral pluralism'.

Roughly speaking, that refers to the fact that apparently good and reasonable human beings seem able to live their lives according to more or less different value systems.

Variety is the spice of life — within limits!

In an unpublished paper, 'Is ethics one or many?', presented to the Association of Teachers of Moral Theology, Gerard J. Hughes examines how it is that apparently good and reasonable people are able to differ on moral issues.

Sometimes people differ about moral issues due to their ignorance of non-moral facts. Some of the empirical information is lacking which is relevant for an accurate evaluation of whether a particular action is conducive to human well-being or not. This may sometimes be the case with new forms of medical treatment. It may be impossible to have accurate information regarding the treatment's long-term effects on human subjects unless one is prepared, having exhausted whatever experimentation might be helpful on non-humans, to take the risk of using this treatment on humans. Hughes would not regard this kind of difference as 'moral pluralism' in the strict sense of the term.

People can also differ on moral issues due to the fact that they hold different philosophical stances which have a bearing on how certain things in life are understood. This is partly the reason why, as we have seen already, there is such radical disagreement on the issue of embryo experimentation. Underlying this disagreement are different philosophical interpretations of personhood and what embryological foundation is needed for us to judge that we are in the presence of a human person. This is another reason why moral disagreements occur. Once again, this is not what Hughes would regard as 'moral pluralism' in the strict sense of the term.

'Moral pluralism' is linked to the phenomenon of cultural pluralism. In different cultures and in different periods of history there can be differing ways of living out our humanity in this world. Down through the ages human beings have tried to achieve personal and social well-being through a rich variety of individual and communal life-styles. Some of these have proved more successful and enduring than others. Some have been better adapted to certain environments or have answered the needs of a particular period in history. Hughes suggests the following thesis for a defensible pluralism in ethics:

There will be as many acceptable moral codes as there are different coherent patterns of true beliefs, and hence of desires which can be successfully satisfied given the nature of the world as it is.

One of the main points Hughes is insisting on is that we can accept 'moral pluralism' without subscribing to moral relativism, which he rejects as false. In other words, to change to the terminology used in the letter of the five Roman Catholic archbishops of England and Wales, to believe in moral pluralism is not to throw overboard 'objective morality'. It is not to reduce morality to the relativity of personal preference.

This is because Hughes believes that as human beings we all share a 'common core of rationality and desires which constitute human nature'. This is the common substratum to the rich variety of human cultures that has existed down through the ages right to the present day. Because of this common substratum, which Hughes calls the 'Principle of Humanity', we are able to engage in moral dialogue across different cultures and are even able, to some extent, to think within another culture. Of course, to recognize this common substratum does not imply that there should be exactly the same moral codes across the various cultures. Hughes makes this point very clearly:

> There will be no one standard by which one might judge the quality of someone's life. There will be no one set of principles governing marriage and family relationships. There will be no one adequate code of justice, no one set of human rights. To be sure, there is a common humanity, and so a common underlying structure to any acceptable moral code, and also to any moral theory. There will be several very general standards of criticism which can be interculturally and interpersonally applied to moralities. That much the principle of humanity guarantees. But the application of these standards of criticism to particular cases will call for the greatest care. Understanding another culture, indeed understanding the life of another human being even within our own culture, is no simple matter. It is a task requiring painstaking empirical study in order to discover just how a particular pattern of behaviour functions in the life of a culture or an individual, just how it is related to the desires and beliefs that are held by that culture or that individual, just how it interacts with the rest of the way of life into which it is integrated. Only when this task of understanding is undertaken will there be any secure basis for comparative moral evaluation. And even when comparative evaluation is possible, the result will be that people living in one moral framework will be able to assimilate and learn from the experience of those living in a different culture: but the result will not be one uniform morality.

As we shall see in Chapter 4 when we are looking at the notion of natural law, 'moral pluralism' as explained by Hughes is completely reconcilable with natural law theory, at least when the latter is purified of some of the grosser accretions of some pre-Vatican II moral theology manuals.

Fundamental moral principles

How does the acceptance of such moral pluralism fit in with the belief in what the five archbishops have described in their letter as 'fundamental moral criteria'? At first sight it might seem that they are referring to more or less the same thing as Hughes's 'Principle of Humanity'.

However, if the five archbishops were to spell out what they mean by 'fundamental moral criteria', they would probably want to go far beyond speaking of a 'common core of rationality and desire which constitute human nature'. No doubt they would want to spell out all that they believe is demanded by the dignity of the human person. They might choose to formulate this in terms of fundamental human rights and duties, as Pope John XXIII did in *Pacem in Terris* (1963), nn. 11–36. Or they might prefer to 'name' the evils of the day, the main and various ways in which human dignity is violated, as did the Council Fathers in *Gaudium et Spes*, n. 27:

> Whatever is opposed to life itself, such as any type of murder, genocide, abortion, euthanasia, or wilful self-destruction, whatever violates the integrity of the human person, such as mutilation, torments inflicted on body or mind, attempts to coerce the will itself; what insults human dignity, such as subhuman living conditions, arbitrary imprisonment, deportation, slavery, prostitution, the selling of women and children; as well as disgraceful working conditions, where people are treated as mere tools for profit, rather than as free and responsible persons; all these things and others of their like are infamies indeed.

This is a far cry from the vague generality of the Principle of Humanity. Yet in itself it is not in conflict with the Principle of Humanity. In fact, far from being in conflict with it, it is actually an attempt to read off its implications within the framework of contemporary culture as perceived by the Council Fathers. This is totally in keeping with the mind-set of *Gaudium et Spes*, which deliberately set out to engage in dialogue with the contemporary world and within that process attempted to read the 'signs of the times'.

Reading the signs of the times could even be described as intelligently listening to the deepest hopes and desires, sufferings and anxieties, of the human family today. That does not seem so very different to the Principle of Humanity's 'common core of rationality and desires which constitute human nature'. Of course, it is one thing to attempt as best one can to formulate the contemporary implications of the Principle of Humanity. It is quite a different thing to claim that one's formulation says all that there is to be said on the issue.

Nevertheless, there can sometimes be more agreement than is often realized over the moral implications of our common humanity. For instance, there are probably few people who would want to describe as *positively good* any of the actions listed by the Council Fathers. That is even true of abortion, which might seem to be one of the most contentious issues on the Vatican II bishops' list. It is interesting that when Archbishop Weakland of Milwaukee held a series of six 'listening sessions' about abortion with groups of women, even though very strong criticisms of the Church's moral teaching were voiced, he was still able to report: 'I did not hear one Catholic woman defend abortion as a good in itself; they all considered it a tragedy in our society, a procedure that no one should have to resort to'. Moreover, the fuller report of the sessions states that no one came to the discussion 'proclaiming herself to be pro-abortion. In the entire six-session discussion and in the hundreds of letters received and read, only one person dismissed abortion as a non-issue and that was not from a woman' (*Origins* (31 May 1990), pp. 33-9). Even Beverly Harrison, whose book *Our Right to Choose* (Boston: Beacon Press, 1983) has been influential in developing a feminist 'Christian ethics' argument for the pro-choice position, would not claim that abortion as such is a good to be celebrated:

> There is no reason for those to us who celebrate procreative choice as a great moral good to pretend that resort to abortion is ever a desirable means of expressing this choice. I know of no one on the pro-choice side who has confused the desirability of the availability of abortion with the celebration of this act in itself. (In Edward Batchelor (ed.), *Abortion: The Moral Issues* (New York: Pilgrim Press, 1982), p. 224)

Hence, she is opposed to 'an abortion culture' and is critical of an abortion industry which exploits women (p. 225).

I suspect that most people would agree with Vatican II's position that, if we are to stand up for the dignity of human persons, we need to spell out as clearly as we can what that means in terms of practical life. They would feel deep in their guts the unacceptability of most of the actions which the bishops condemn as violations of human dignity. Some might want to add a gloss with regard to the trio of abortion, euthanasia and wilful self-destruction. They might not want to defend these as human 'goods' but they might want to ensure that the condemnation of these as 'infamies' would not imply a judgement of moral condemnation on persons who resorted to these actions in certain tragic situations.

One common culture?

A further question has to be faced. Living as we do today in what is called the 'global village', does this mean that in the world today there is a common culture shared by all of us? Certainly, largely due to the explosion of the communications media and the increased facility of international travel, there is now a global consciousness such as never has existed previously in the history of the human race. Moreover, this has brought about not simply an awareness of our global interdependence but has even caused this global inter-dependence to increase. *Our Common Future*, the title of the 1987 World Commission on Environment and Development ('Brundt-land') Report, is a striking expression of this global interdependence and the actual contents of the report spell it out in very great detail. For instance, the Report states:

> Until recently, the planet was a large world in which human activities and their effects were neatly compartmentalized within nations, within sectors (energy, agriculture, trade), and within broad areas of concern (environmental, economic, social). These compartments have begun to dissolve. This applies in particular to the various global 'crises' that have seized public concern, particularly over the past decade. These are not separate crises: an environmental crisis, a development crisis, an energy crisis. They are all one. (p. 4)

John Paul II seems to adopt a similar analysis in his 1991 encyclical *Centesimus Annus*: 'Today we are facing the so-called "globaliza-tion" of the economy, a phenomenon which is not to be dismissed, since it can create unusual opportunities for greater prosperity' (n. 58).

Although there is some sort of world culture in existence at present, this does not prevent the continued existence of a variety of more particular cultures based on a common national, ethnic, racial or religious identity. This would seem to be borne out by the increasing emphasis placed by Christian Churches on the notion of inculturation. This means having a respect for local cultures and recognizing their uniqueness and the particular riches they bring to human and Christian living.

What about a common morality for the human family? It could be argued that the 1948 United Nations Declaration on Human Rights was an attempt to articulate some kind of common acceptance of basic human values. The same might be true of the category of 'crimes against humanity' which lay at the centre of the post-war Nuremberg trials. However, I would prefer to see these as similar to *Gaudium et Spes*, n. 26. They are attempts to put more flesh and blood on what Hughes called 'the Principle of Humanity'. Like the Vatican II statement, they are substantial statements of major importance. However, that does not mean that they are the last word on the subject.

Consistency and dialogue

A recent development in the public presentation of Roman Catholic moral teaching has been Cardinal Bernardin's emphasis on the need for what he calls a 'consistent life ethic'. By that he means that any-one who claims to be 'pro-life' must not be selective as regards those whose lives are not being properly respected. He has given a number of major addresses on this theme. The following quotation from an address at Seattle University (2 March 1986) gives a taste of what he is trying to say:

> If one contends, as we do, that the right of every fetus to be born should be protected by civil law and supported by civil consensus, then our moral, political and economic responsibilities do not stop at the moment of birth. Those who defend the right to life of the weakest among us must be equally visible in support of the quality of life of the powerless among us: the old and the young, the hungry and the homeless, the undocu-mented immigrant and the unemployed worker. Such a quality-of-life posture translates into specific political and economic positions on tax policy, employment generation, welfare policy, nutrition and feeding programs, and health care. Consistency means we cannot have it both ways: we cannot urge a compassionate society and vigorous public policy to protect the rights of the unborn and then argue that compassion and significant public programs on behalf of the needy undermine the

moral fiber of the society or are beyond the proper scope of govern-
mental responsibility. (*Origins* (20 March 1986), p. 657)

It is interesting to note that Hughes, in his 'Is ethics one or many?'
paper referred to above, highlights 'coherence' as an essential mark
of any ethic that claims to be humanly satisfactory. Presumably this
is because coherence is a requirement of reasonable thinking.

However, what Cardinal Bernardin is calling for is not just a
Christian ethic that is consistent. He is demanding that its consistency be judged by its stance on issues where respect for *human life* is
involved. This emphasis is reflected in groups claiming to support
the 'pro-life' cause, though not all such groups show the same concern for consistency on all life issues as Cardinal Bernardin. This
was one of the issues highlighted by Archbishop Weakland in his
response to the listening sessions with women on abortion mentioned earlier. Not only were women challenging the Church to
'maintain more consistency between its teaching and its actions'.
The pro-life movement itself came under considerable criticism: 'It
was felt that life was not consistently held in the same esteem after
birth by some in that group'. Many of the women also felt angered
by the Church's stand on birth control, believing it to be inconsistent
with the Church's championing of the dignity of the human person.
Weakland noted 'how far the gap is between the official teaching
in this area and its non-receptivity by some very conscientious
women'. For him this non-acceptance was symbolized by one
woman's comment: 'We want to be pro-choice before conception'.

The notion of a 'consistent life ethic' sounds very positive and
attractive. Nevertheless, it is not without its problems. For instance,
does it imply that respect for life is the core value in any human
morality? If so, how do we handle a conflict between the respect
owed to the lives of different persons or when what might be
regarded as another basic value is at stake, for example, the safety of
the community? Moreover, what about the dignity of the human
person which, according to Vatican II, lies at the very heart of
Christian morality? Is a pro-life ethic simply another name for a
person-centred ethic? This needs to be clarified because some
approaches to medical care have so emphasized the preservation of
life that they have disregarded the deepest needs of the human persons they are supposed to be caring for. Richard McCormick mentions a letter he received claiming that some New York nursing
homes were 'concentration camps' and did not let the elderly die

with dignity. The writer instanced a 93-year-old senile but physically alert woman who had given up eating and so a feeding tube was inserted against which she fought 'tooth and nail with the most awful expression of fear'. She was then tied to the bed to stop her moving the tube — and for some patients this indignity continues for years! The letter continues: 'It's really a wonderful way of breaking a person's spirit if she has any left at that point' (*The Critical Calling* (Georgetown, 1989), p. 386). According to British law, removal of a nasogastric tube in the case of someone in a persistent vegetative state would be treated *prima facie* as murder, even though the family, doctors and chaplain agree that this should be done since the tube is giving no real human benefit to the patient who is, in fact, being prevented from dying by this artificial medical procedure. Incidentally, as John Paris notes, the family's decision here would have the backing of traditional Catholic teaching (cf. McCormick, p. 376).

Furthermore, if a pro-life ethic and a person-centred ethic are the same thing, where does this leave the official Roman Catholic position in the debate on embryo research? Cardinal Hume has spoken out very strongly in favour of what he calls 'the traditional Christian vision of the sanctity of human life' and he has stoutly defended the full human 'dignity and rights under the law' of that life, regardless of whether it 'can, from day one, be regarded as a person and whether it is already endowed with an immortal soul'. These are powerful assertions but they leave us with a problem since they seem to assert absolute respect for human life even in the absence of a human person as the subject of that life.

One of the main assumptions of this book is that the basic foundation of Christian morality lies in the God-given dignity of the human person, seen, of course, in relation to the rest of God's creation. Christian morality should claim to be *pro-person* rather than *pro-life*. We now need to explore further what is involved in the expression, 'the dignity of the human person'. That is the theme of the next chapter.

Chapter 3

THE DIGNITY OF THE HUMAN PERSON:
A COMMON STARTING-POINT

In 1987 the Church of England Board for Social Responsibility (BSR) produced a study entitled *Changing Britain: Social Diversity and Moral Unity*. This report examined the phenomenon of social diversity in Britain and attempted to search beneath the surface for the common values which it believed cemented the country's unity in the face of this diversity. It located this moral unity in a basic belief in the dignity of the human person, a dignity which is essentially bound up with interrelatedness to other human persons and to the rest of creation. Consequently, it focused on the community dimension of personal existence and recognized that this was an intrinsic element in human flourishing:

> It is difficult to give any content to the sense of person without taking into account the presence of other persons with whom one is in relationship. *Interrelatedness* seems to be integral to the development of the promise contained in the concept of personhood . . . Personhood, for its flourishing, seems to require other persons in a relationship which is typified by freedom and is expressed in mutuality, in equality of respect, and in solidarity. Morality, thus understood, is essentialy a matter of respect for persons and the necessary conditions for their flourishing. (nn. 55–56)

A few paragraphs later the report notes but rejects the objection that a person-centred ethic 'does not seem to give value to the natural order in its own right': 'It is not hard to see that a "person" ethic must extend to embrace the whole set of relationships in which human beings stand, including their relationship with their environment, and must respect the rest of God's creatures and creation' (n. 59).

Moreover, while insisting that a truly human morality is founded on this common basis of 'the dignity of the human person', the report emphasizes that 'it is not a static concept': 'Moral codes, or human identikits, have a dynamic element to them, as history uncovers or recovers apparently fresh aspects of what it is, desirably, to be human' (n. 54). It also points out that such a common basis 'leaves plenty of scope for disagreement' (n. 56).

'The dignity of the human person' is also the foundational value found in the moral teaching of Vatican II, as the BSR report notes. It is enunciated in a number of the Council's documents and lies at the heart of *Gaudium et Spes* (cf. nn. 3, 12, 35 and 76). Furthermore, the Universal Declaration of Human Rights, while being formulated by a secular institution in deliberately non-religious language, is still based on the recognition that 'these rights derive from the inherent dignity of the human person'.

In this chapter I hope to explore more fully what precisely is implied in this moral criterion of the dignity of the human person.

Fundamental moral principles based on the dignity of the human person

The Roman Catholic archbishops of England and Wales in their letter to *The Times* stated their 'conviction that fundamental moral criteria are absolute and cannot depend on the personal preferences of individuals'. I would interpret this assertion as claiming that fundamental moral principles are true independently of whether we choose to believe them or not. Whether 'absolute' is an appropriate word for expressing what they wanted to say might be questioned. However, their insistence on the truth of fundamental moral principles is in no doubt.

In this assertion they are aligning themselves with a moral tradition which pre-dates Christianity itself. One of its founders whose thought still commands enormous respect today is the Greek philosopher Aristotle. Hugo Meynell, a present-day exponent of this tradition, sums up Aristotle's position as follows:

> Aristotelianism is at bottom a systematic realization of the insight that 'genuine objectivity is the fruit of authentic subjectivity', as a great modern Aristotelian (Bernard Lonergan) has expressed it; that good morality and good politics are a matter of intelligent and reasonable action in an environment to be intelligently and reasonably apprehended; and that there are objective norms to be articulated and followed which lead to fulfilment in the lives of human individuals and societies. ('On being an Aristotelian', *Heythrop Journal* (1991), p. 245)

It may be that the forcefulness of the archbishops' proclamation of this moral tradition is because they share the fears of Alasdair MacIntyre. In his celebrated work *After Virtue*, MacIntyre laments the demise of this tradition in popular thinking and claims that the prevailing moral climate in the West is precisely that denounced by the archbishops. In other words, what matters ethically is what people 'feel' (hence it is called 'emotivism'). Moral statements simply express our personal preferences and make no claim to truth.

The moral tradition to which the archbishops are nailing their colours (and in this, not surprisingly, they are at one with Vatican II) is called 'realism' in current philosophical parlance. It asserts that the truth entailed in moral statements is a truth which is not dependent on our personal beliefs. In fact, 'realism' is recognized as a very coherent and substantial position among modern thinkers in the field of philosophical ethics. This ties in with the increasing respectability of natural law thinking at present. Natural law thinking, properly understood (cf. Chapter 4), provides a very coherent and well-argued version of 'realism' in moral thinking.

I think there is no doubt that *Gaudium et Spes* was based on a mind-set which embraced 'realism' in the field of morality. After insisting that in decision-making on responsible parenthood 'the moral aspect of any procedure does not depend solely on sincere intentions or an evaluation of motives', the Council Fathers stated that 'it must be determined by objective standards'. Their understanding of 'objective standards' is clearly a realist one since they go on to say that these objective standards are 'based on the nature of the human person and his acts'.

The precise wording of this passage came under the closest scrutiny by the bishops. In its penultimate version it used the expression 'objective criteria based on the dignity of the human person'. A few of the bishops were unhappy with this. They still clung to the notion that sexual actions, being generative and thus species-orientated, had a finality of their own distinct from the human persons involved. They wanted this included in the text. Hence they suggested that the text be changed in such a way that there would be two distinct criteria proposed: (1) the nature of the human person; and (2) the nature of the action itself. The drafting committee turned down this amendment on the grounds that it would substantially alter the meaning of the text and at this late stage the conciliar procedure did not allow substantial alterations to be made. As a good-will gesture (and no doubt in the hope of getting the proposers' votes for the final text) the drafting committee included mention of 'acts' in the final version. However, the wording was such that it was clear that 'acts' were in no way seen as a criterion distinct from the person. Rather their moral relevance flowed from the fact that they were the acts *of the human person*. The official Latin text brings this out much more clearly than the English translation.

Furthermore, the comment of the drafting committee on this passage stated that it was enunciating a 'general principle'. Hence, it is a principle which applies to the whole field of human morality. It formulates this basic principle as follows: 'Human activity must be judged insofar as it refers to the human person integrally and adequately considered' (*Acta Synodalia Concilii Vaticani II*, vol. IV, part 7, p. 502, n. 37). In other words, the morality of human actions has to be determined by reference to the human persons involved. This is not just a reference to the good intention of the person acting. Without dismissing that as irrelevant, it is stressing the necessity of basing one's moral evaluation on the good, integrally and adequately considered, of all the persons involved.

The good of the human person, integrally and adequately considered

One of the writers who has gone most thoroughly into the meaning of this key phrase of the drafting committee is Louis Janssens in his article 'Artificial insemination: ethical considerations' (*Louvain Studies* (1980), pp. 3–29). He takes this phrase to refer to the 'fundamental and constant aspects or dimensions of the person'. However, he is careful to insist that these dimensions, though they can be delineated and analysed individually, cannot be separated one from another: 'These aspects or dimensions belong to one and the same human person: they are interwoven and form a synthesis because each is proper to the integrity of every person' (p. 4).

Janssens suggests that there are eight such fundamental dimensions of the human person. The human person is (1) a subject; (2) an embodied subject; (3) part of the material world; (4) interrelational with other persons; (5) an interdependent social being; (6) historical; (7) equal but unique; (8) called to know and worship God. Taken together these essential dimensions constitute 'the human person integrally and adequately considered'. Whatever promotes or violates the good of the human person considered in this comprehensive way is respectively morally right or wrong. This is the basic criterion for a person-centred morality as put forward by Vatican II.

Of course, there may be other equally or even more valid ways of analysing the various dimensions of being a human person. However, I have found Janssens' analysis helpful and enlightening. Hence, I have decided to use his eight dimensions as the general framework for my basic presentation of person-centred morality in this chapter.

1 The human person is a subject

This ties in with Kant's insistence that human persons may not be treated as mere 'means'. As subject, the human person, writes Janssens, 'is normally called to be conscious, to act according to his conscience, in freedom and in a responsible manner' (p. 5).

In his book *Christian Morality: The Word becomes Flesh* (Georgetown/Gill & Macmillan, 1987), Josef Fuchs recounts a very thought-provoking Hassidic legend: 'Before his death Rabbi Sussja said: "In the world to come, I will not be asked, 'Why were you not Moses?' I will be asked, 'Why were you not Sussja?'"' (p. 143). This brings out in a very striking manner the 'subject' dimension of being a human person. In the final analysis, a person is responsible not only for what he or she does, but also far more profoundly for who he or she is. That is why freedom is so fundamental to this dimension of the human person. Moreover, in the first instance it does not mean simply freedom to choose. It means freedom to be — to accept oneself and to become oneself. We shall return to this basic level of freedom in our consideration of sin, forgiveness and conversion in Chapter 7. Obviously, too, it has a bearing on the uniqueness of the human person which is considered later in this chapter under the seventh dimension.

Our traditional understanding of morality takes this 'subject' dimension as its starting-point. Morality is about our responsibility for what we do and the kind of person we choose to become. That is why a certain minimum level of freedom and understanding have always been taken as pre-requisites for moral responsibility.

This dimension of the human person had profound implications for practical living in a whole variety of areas of human life. In medical ethics, for instance, it grounds the necessity of informed consent before any medical intervention is permitted. In social ethics it is the basis of our rejection of any form of totalitarianism and it also provides a critical point of reference for assessing what level of social intervention is humanly acceptable in different situations. Linked to this 'subject' dimension are such foundational social values as 'one person, one vote', participation, the basic freedoms of the individual person, etc. It also ties in with the emphasis so many people lay on their national identity. For them this is an important aspect of their personal identity and so national self-determination is seen by them as bound up with their own freedom as individual persons.

This 'subject' dimension of being a human person ties in, too, with some of the major themes being brought to our attention by women theologians. For instance, it undergirds the struggle of women to get their moral agency fully recognized and it also links in with their emphasis on 'empowerment'. This will be treated more fully in Chapter 5.

When we consider the possibilities of actually altering our basic human make-up that human technology is opening up, this dimension points to a practical principle of the utmost importance. Any development which diminishes our capacity to be free human agents reduces us as human persons. Hence, such a development would be dehumanizing and thus immoral. As well as being true at an individual level, this might also have implications for social policy. For instance, the development of genetic engineering might give rise to the possibility of producing offspring with so-called 'superior' genetic endowments. Such 'superior' characteristics might only serve to isolate these people from the rest of the human family. The level of 'subjectivity' they might demand for themselves could perhaps only be achieved through the diminishment of others as 'subjects'.

2 *The human person is an embodied subject*

Embodiment is a crucial dimension of our personal being. Throughout Christian tradition there has been a constant temptation to neglect this dimension and to move in the direction of dualism in some form or other. In contradiction to the unifying vision of Aristotle, the soul has been presented almost as a self-sufficient entity, dwelling in the body. This is very different to the teaching of Aquinas, as José Comblin has pointed out:

> In St Thomas's teaching, the soul is the only substantial form of the human being, and hence the substantial form of the body itself. The soul has no kind of existence apart from the body. The human being is composed of matter and form, not of body and soul . . . The body is matter, but it is also form or soul; and the soul is form, but it is also matter, or body. The body is soul, and the soul is body. (José Comblin, *Being*

Human: A Christian Anthropology, Liberation and Theology 6 (Burns & Oates, 1990), pp. 63-4)

He goes on to lament that 'not even the Thomists remained faithful to their great doctor's teaching'. Their dualism made it possible for them to justify such gross violations of the dignity of the human person as slavery or torture by the Inquisition. Comblin notes: 'All of this was possible only because, for theologians, the body was not the real human being. To torture the body, to deprive the body of its liberty, could be justified, since the body was somehow external to the human person, and its mere instrument' (p. 64).

This denial of our essential embodiment has even distorted our understanding of human freedom. We have tended to look for some hidden aspect of ourselves where we are completely undetermined and to locate human freedom at that point. In reality our freedom is embodied freedom. In other words, it is precisely through our bodies that we are able to be free. What we sometimes refer to as our 'limitations' are in fact simply the current boundaries of our present abilities. They are the package of gifts we have to live our lives with. The formative influences on our lives have not had the effect of reducing our freedom but rather of giving us more embodied freedom to work with. That is particularly true of a good education. It does not deprive us of our freedom. It extends the parameters within which our freedom is able to operate. It is 'liberating' in the literal sense of the word.

How we relate to our bodies has often been envisaged as a struggle either to rise above the passionate movement of our bodily senses or else to dominate these unruly bodily passions. The negative approach to anger that has been common in Christian teaching typifies this quasi-denial of our essential embodiment. Introducing a special issue of *The Way* on this topic, the editor makes the perceptive comment:

The blanket negative judgements on anger of our childhood and schooling and the lack of education in the creative use of it have had harmful consequences. Expressions of anger were unacceptable, so repression, under the guise of rigid 'self-control', was often the only counsel we received. Our anger, instead of being acknowledged and accepted, went underground. There it festered, causing depression, erupting from time to time in unforeseen, uncontrolled explosions and marring our behaviour in hidden ways we did not fully recognize, still less understand. And because we held anger to be sinful, these angry feelings and the explosions they caused led us more deeply into guilt, from which there seemed no escape. All this contains its own destructive logic: to be angry is wrong and displeasing to God; yet not to be angry is impossible, for there is so much in the world that makes us so. (David Lonsdale, 'Slow to anger', *The Way* (1990), p. 88)

A similar point is made by Beverly Wildung Harrison, as we shall see when we examine the special contribution of women theologians, who lay great emphasis on the dimension of embodiment.

This same dualism, with its downgrading of the body, has had a very detrimental effect on the development of a healthy Christian theology of sexuality and marriage. In the early centuries of the Church through such influences as Stoic thought which, according to John Noonan, 'was in the air the intellectual converts to Christianity breathed' (*Contraception*, Harvard University Press, 1965, p. 46), many Christian writers gradually lost the healthy appreciation of the body which was part of the Jewish tradition, expressed so beautifully in the celebration of human erotic sexual love in the Song of Songs. The Stoics distrusted the emotions, including feelings of joy or pleasure. Reason, self-control and purpose were what mattered to them. Passion in marriage, as elsewhere, was suspect. As Noonan says, 'Marriage had to have another basis. Plainly that basis was its necessary part in the propagation of the race. By this standard of rational purposefulness, self-evident and supplied by nature, excess in marital intercourse might be measured' (p. 46). Hence, marital intercourse was morally right only if its purpose was for the begetting of children. If this was not a couple's intention, it stood condemned as 'unreasonable' and therefore beneath their human dignity. In keeping with this criterion, intercourse during pregnancy was also regarded as irrational and hence inhuman.

Although these early Christian writers recognized the goodness of the love of married couples, they did not see this love as being in any way celebrated or communicated through the shared joy of sexual intercourse. This is even true of St Augustine, despite his very exalted notion of the spiritual love of husband and wife. Far from being expressed in their sexual union, this love is degraded by intercourse, since they are mutually dragged down to the level of their animal nature, even though excusably so if it is for the sake of having children. This complete separation of married love and sexual intercourse is even more marked when Augustine speaks of the place of children in a marrriage. Nowhere does he speak of them as the fruit of their parents' married love. They are the fruit of intercourse but not of love (e.g. *De bono conjugali*, n. 1).

This distortion of a healthy appreciation of the goodness of human sexuality has dogged Christian theology down through the centuries, even though there have been glimmers of light at various times. The result has been that Christianity has never really developed a theology of embodied relationship and a healthy sexual ethic flowing from such a theology. The focus of any theological thinking about sexuality that has gone on has been influenced by the concerns of canon law. Hence, it has been confined within the contract model of marriage and has tended to concentrate on the procreational dimension of the marriage act and its implications for the marriage contract. Even there it is only very gradually that a much more positive appreciation of the importance of the sexual relationship within a marriage has emerged. Moreover, at least a good measure of the credit for that must go once again to 'foreign prophets' like Sigmund Freud and D. H. Lawrence.

All this has changed now, thanks to Vatican II. *Gaudium et Spes* very explicitly celebrates the goodness of the sexual love of married people, which it recognizes to be 'eminently human', involving 'the good of the whole person' and enriching 'the expressions of body and mind' with a special dignity. It sees this love as 'merging the human with the divine' and acknowledges that it is 'uniquely expressed and perfected through the marital act'. It also recognizes that married love expressed in this way has the power to 'signify and promote that mutual self-giving by which spouses enrich each other with a joyful and thankful will' (all quotations from n. 49). St Augustine could never have accepted such teaching, though I suspect that were he alive today, with his powers of perception and his feel for the current signs of the times, he would probably be delighted and would have been one of the leading figures in this move for a much more positive appreciation of human sexuality.

Nevertheless, it needs to be recognized that some of the more positive teaching of Vatican II on marriage was being proclaimed by some other Christian Churches years before the Council. For example, already in 1939 the Methodist Conference was celebrating the multi-dimensional God-given goodness of sex in the lives of human persons:

> . . . sex is intended, in the purpose of God, to be a blessing and a joy to mankind . . . The impulses and instincts of sex which men and women share with the animal creation have been exalted to something higher in human love, and from the beginning the love of man and woman has been used to build up the fellowship of mankind.

The influence of sex, indeed, goes far beyond the creation of the family. It is one of the chief sources of living energy in men and women, the expression of which cannot be limited to the physical side of marriage . . . From the impulses of sex and its associated parental and filial instincts arise those sentiments and emotions of love, tenderness and sympathy, which inspire and direct so much of our moral life. The awakening of love heightens our appreciation of whatever in this world is beautiful and good. (*The Christian View of Marriage and the Family*, Statement adopted at 1939 Methodist Conference, I, i)

Similar developments had been taking place in pre-conciliar Roman Catholic writing on marriage. For example, on the goodness of the shared joy of sexual love-making in marriage it would be hard to better the writing of the married layman Justin Gosling in his book *Marriage and the Love of God* (Geoffrey Chapman), published in 1965 (only in December of that year did the Council Fathers finalize the text of *Gaudium et Spes* on marriage):

The desire for intercourse . . . is a desire to share intimacy, to give pleasure, to express joy, to show vividly the love one bears one's partner. It is important that this should be an enjoyable activity, and an important part of the enjoyment is the accompanying physical sensations . . . If you ask a married man why he has intercourse with his wife, he is likely to be a little surprised, and may well answer 'Because I enjoy it, of course'. It would be a mistake, however, to take this answer as meaning that his sole or dominant motive was his own gratification . . . It may be the answer of a man puzzled by the question . . . Viewing intercourse as making love, and so good, he takes the question as suggesting that still some extra inducement is needed; he is declaring that he needs no special persuasion to declare his love, he enjoys doing it . . . It is important, then, that intercourse should be enjoyed and that it should mean something to the partners as a sign of their mutual devotion. (pp. 62–3)

My own belief — which I cannot substantiate — is that many married Christians down through the ages would have said 'Amen' to what Gosling has written. I find it hard to believe that, despite the negative writings of non-married male theologians, ordinary men and women were not experiencing in their own love for each other at least a partial realization of the truth Gosling is writing about — provided, of course, their relationship was able to attain a moderate level of mutuality, despite the corrosive force of the patriarchal structures of their day.

A deeper appreciation of this essential dimension of embodiment lies at the heart of current discussions about the morality of genital expression of love in a homosexual relationship. Some would argue that biological sex organs are determinative of personal sexual orientation. Hence, homosexual acts are disordered personal acts and so immoral. Others would argue that personal sexual orientation is a much more complex reality. They would hold that whether a person's sexual orientation turns out to be heterosexual or homosexual, the same basic principles governing the morality of sexual relationships apply. That is the position found in the report *A Christian Understanding of Human Sexuality*, submitted to the Methodist Conference in 1980 (cf. sections C. 20 and E. 49). It was reiterated in the revised version of the report presented to the 1982 Conference:

> [Some Christians, including a majority of the Working Party] hold . . . that heterosexual and homosexual relationships alike are to be valued according to the presence or absence of love as the New Testament describes it. They agree that for some homosexual people (as for some heterosexual people) celibacy is a vocation, and that for others a choice between a partnership without physical expression and one that includes genital expression within a committed relationship is to be accepted as a choice which Christians may responsibly make. (n. 52)

3 As an embodied subject the human person is part of the material world

This dimension of our being a human person raises the question of our standing *vis-à-vis* the rest of the material world. There is no doubt that as human persons we depend on the rest of material creation. We cannot live without air to breathe, water to drink, food to eat. We need warmth and shelter. We constitute a major element in natural ecosystems. Moreover, the undulating history of civilization is a story of the progressive transformation of 'nature' into technology and culture. Moving from an early stage of hunters and gatherers, 'discovering' fire and 'inventing' the wheel, we have gradually unearthed the hidden potentialities of the rest of material creation. We have developed new forms of energy, communications, transport, construction materials, etc. Human technology has gone far beyond the standard way the ordinary operations of natural activity work. We have not only been able to appreciate the beauty of the natural world; we have also been able to use material things to create new forms of beauty in art and architecture, in music and literature.

Moreover, this relationship is not just one of our dependence on the rest of the material world. Increasingly the rest of the material world is becoming dependent on us for its survival. In us our world has developed the power of self-destruction or at least of bringing to an end the continuation of higher forms of life on our planet. On the other hand, the Orthodox theologian John D. Zizioulas suggests that in us lies the only hope of our world transcending its finitude and being elevated to eternal survival ('Preserving God's creation: three lectures on theology and ecology', *King's Theological Review* (1989), pp. 1–5, 41–5; (1990), pp. 1–5). At a less profound level than this, the rest of the material world is being more and more affected by the way the human family chooses to live. There is no doubt, therefore, that our relationship with the rest of creation is one of interdependence and that this interdependence is a fundamental dimension of being a human person.

A consciousness of this interdependence has in recent years given rise to a new branch of ethics, ecological ethics. This discipline is still in its early days. In the course of trying to articulate practical principles for human behaviour it is wrestling with such basic questions as how a person-centred ethic can really respect the intrinsic value of the rest of creation. It is also exploring the political ramifications of an ecological ethics. In a paper entitled 'The changing paradigms of sin', delivered to the Catholic Theological Association of Great Britain (printed in *New Blackfriars* (1989), pp. 489–97), I tried to highlight the ethical dimension of our interdependence with the rest of creation:

> Humanity is bound up in an intrinsic and essential relationship of inter-dependence with the rest of creation. There are not two separate and independent ethical criteria operating in ecological issues, what is good for humanity and what is good for creation as a whole. To consider creation as a whole is to consider it as including humanity. It is to recognize humanity as creation reaching a higher level of existence, the level of personal and social consciousness. This level of existence does not constitute a breaking away from the rest of creation. Creational health remains an integral element of the good of humanity, just as does bodily health. And vice-versa. In other words, the health of the rest of creation is now dependent on humanity conducting itself in a way which befits its place and responsibility within the whole of creation. Humanity can be a cancerous growth within creation — and some 'deep ecologists' believe it is such already. Or it can be creation reaching out to a yet higher level of life in which it can articulate its hymn of praise and thanksgiving to its creator and reflect in its very way of living the deeply personal and

holistic life of its creator. For humanity to distance itself from the rest of creation and lord it over it would be a form of alienation from an integral part of ourselves. (p. 497)

In keeping with the basic theme of this book, it should be noted that this growth in ecological consciousness has arisen out of the common concern of the human family and has subsequently made its way into the more explicit teaching of the Church. At the time of the Council, ecological concerns were not yet universally seen to be one of the signs of the times. Hence, the Council's vision of human interrelatedness was deficient in its awareness of how this extended to the rest of creation. Incidentally, the fact that humanity's increasing awareness of the urgency of ecological issues has had a 'consciousness-raising' impact on the Church itself offers a striking example of a major theme of this book, namely, that the Church needs to listen to prophets outside the Church if it is to grasp the implications of the Gospel for today. Edward Schillebeeckx made this point particularly with regard to social ethics in his book *God the Future of Man* (Sheed & Ward, 1969):

> The past has shown that, long before the churches had analyzed the social problems, there were people who, in their commitment and in a preanalytic dialogue with the world, had already reached the moral decision that fundamental changes were required. New situational ethical imperatives have rarely or never been initiated by philosophers, theologians, churches or ecclesiastical authorities. They emerge from a concrete experience of life and impose themselves with the clear evidence of experience . . . The church cannot fulfill her prophetic task with regard to the worldly problems of man and society simply by appealing to revelation, but only by listening very carefully to that 'foreign prophecy' which appeals to her from the situation of the world and in which she recognizes the familiar voice of her Lord. (p. 163)

It should not surprise us, therefore, that 1987 marks the first occasion any proper attention is given to ecological concerns in a papal encyclical, i.e. John Paul II's *Sollicitudo Rei Socialis*, n. 34. Clearly the Pope has recognized 'the familiar voice of his Lord' in the growing ecological awareness among people as he returns to the same theme with remarkable force in his message for the 1990 World Day of Peace and then develops it still further in *Centesimus Annus* (1991), where he links it to a concern for 'an authentic human ecology' (n. 38). The message regarding the importance of ecological concerns, having been picked up from 'foreign prophets', is obviously destined to become an essential element in Catholic social teaching.

In recent years our affinity with the rest of the material world has added enormously to our understanding of how we operate as human beings. It was the belief of Aristotle, shared by Aquinas, that human beings began life in the womb initially in the vegetative state, then progressed through the animal state and finally reached the stage of humanity. Although interpreting the human significance of early embryological development is still a matter of intense debate, Aristotle's view hardly does justice to modern scientific knowledge. Nevertheless, at the level of the development of our species there is some similarity between Aristotle's notion and modern evolutionary theory. Moreover, this 'part of the material world' dimension we are considering forces us to recognize our fundamental connection, not merely with the vegetative and animal world, but even with the rest of the material world. Human persons are not just composed of living cells; those living cells are themselves made up of a highly intricate arrangement of various molecules, atoms and even subatomic matter.

Brendan Lovett, in his book *On Earth as in Heaven: Corresponding to God in Philippine Context* (Quezon City, Philippines: Claretian Publications, 1988), explores much more thoroughly this dimension of our personal being. In his analysis of what is meant by 'integral human good', he quite deliberately begins at what some people might regard as the wrong end. His five most basic levels of human value are respectively physical, chemical, botanical, zoological and vital. Only after establishing this basic foundation does he then move on to consider the more specifically human levels — social (i.e. political, economic, technological), cultural, personal and religious.

In introducing this analysis 'from below' he writes:

> If it is true that 'differentiation and creativity flow from below upwards', then the 'bottom' level of value (physical value) is the appropriate place to begin. And appropriation of this first level is crucial. Human beings are the point where the emergent process of the universe comes to consciousness. This means that who we are is the consciousness of the universe. To fail to identify ourselves with the twenty billion year old story of our emergent universe is to remain incapable of ever approximating to the human good. The very first step in moving towards the integral human good is being reconciled to and glorying in the story of the universe as our foundational truth. (p. 21)

His treatment of the zoological level of human value is also worth quoting:

> Life comes to be only as a web of life, as interconnected life forms which can only survive through symbiosis . . . Everybody knows that sooner or later destruction of the web of life must mean the end of human life. Reverence for life in all its manifestations — all being interconnected — is a condition of our survival. We can only hope to relate in a truly human way towards each other if we have a respect for life which goes beyond the human to embrace all the creatures that together constitute the possibility of our emergence into life and the sustaining ground of our continued existence on this planet. (p. 24)

This is a timely reminder to us that life itself is a prerequisite for our being able to enjoy any dimensions of the good of the human person. It is a foundational good. That is why there is surely something badly out of order in the way we are living as a human family when we are prepared to devote most of our resources into promoting the more refined technological and cultural goods of our modern ages (improving communications, transport, developing high-technology medical care or sophisticated weaponry, etc.), while so many in our world are being denied the foundational value of life itself. There may perhaps be grounds for disagreement as to whether an early human embryo has the status of a human person and hence its life is owed the same respect as the life of any other human person. But there are no grounds for denying that the millions of people, mainly women and children, starving throughout the world are human persons.

Moreover, if we hold a view of rights that insists that rights are meaningless without corresponding claims or obligations, I would suggest that each person's right to life constitutes a primary claim on the rest of the human family — and most particularly on that society, or group, or those individuals who form that person's most immediate web of interdependence. This highlights the need for accurate social analysis. Social analysis, uncovering the interlocking strands of the web of interdependence, may very quickly lead us to people and places not necessarily in the immediate vicinity of the persons whose lives are threatened. Enda McDonagh, in his book *Social Ethics and the Christian*, gives a very striking example of how this linkage can have wider and wider ramifications in our modern world:

> . . . it is impossible to present a balanced and comprehensive view of medical ethics without taking into account the food, nutrition and

hygienic needs of people, with implications for the distribution of resources and effect on the environment, with their implications for population growth, the structure of international trade or the standard of living of the affluent societies with their international and national political ramifications.

Taking a different line within the same area of medical ethics — the use and abuse of drugs goes far beyond any immediate code of prescription for the individual into the whole world of the drug industry, multinational corporations, animal and human experimentation, adequate testing and safeguards, fair and unfair advertising, provision of doctors and other medical personnel, the meaning of health, the significance of pain, quality of life, attitudes to the dying and to death . . . (p. 11)

This 'part of the material world' level of our personal being is, of course, not an argument for bigger and bigger families — the more life the better! The human species is not exempt from Lovett's warning that 'any species multiplied to excess becomes a horror'. Nor does the 'part of the material world' dimension of our personal being justify a 'keep alive at any cost' approach. Life may be a foundational good but the other human goods built on its foundation go to make up the quality of life. To fight against the normal human dying process when the quality of life has become virtually sub-human is to mistake the place of physical life as a dimension of the good of the human person. To believe that life is the foundation for other human goods does not imply that it is an absolute value, to be defended at all costs even in the absence of any other dimensions of human good. After all, Christians have always accepted that other goods related to the human person (e.g. love, friendship, religious faith) can be valued more than life and hence a person may sacrifice his or her life for these goods.

Christian morality is pro-person more than pro-life. Disconcerted by the very narrow interpretation of 'pro-life' by some Catholics, Cardinal Bernardin, as we have seen already, has been the tireless advocate of what he calls a 'consistent life-ethic'. I would suggest that a more appropriate description of his position would be a 'consistent person-ethic'.

4 The human person is essentially interrelational with other human persons

Developmental psychology has made us much more aware that we can only develop as human persons who are embodied subjects through relationship with other embodied human subjects. Increased understanding of the processes which take place in the early years of a child's development has made us recognize that it is crucially important that the relationship of a young child with the significant 'other(s)' in his or her life needs to be one of embodied tenderness and personal security. Eric Fuchs, in his book *Sexual Desire and Love: Origin and History of the Christian Ethic of Sexuality and Marriage* (James Clarke, 1983), makes this the launching pad for his whole elaboration of a theology of sexuality. He points out that my personal growth and maturation involves coming to experience and accept myself as a distinct person (recognizing my differentiation from others) and also recognizing that other persons really are other and not just extensions of myself. The outcome of this experience is that I am gradually able to relate to the other without losing myself or without devouring the other. He insists that our human sexuality is the medium through which we achieve this key developmental experience, beginning with our initial bodily experiences of self *vis-à-vis* our parents, especially our mother. Hence, Fuchs is able to speak of our sexuality as a means to our humanization. In a powerful passage commenting on the 'two becoming one flesh' text in Genesis 2:24, Fuchs argues that human sexuality draws its prime meaning from the basic truth that as persons we are interrelational beings:

> . . . sexuality concerns first of all the realm of relationship and is not primarily biological. Man and woman become one not primarily to procreate children but to encounter one another in the unique manner where, through sexuality, something of the ultimate mystery of human life, as God calls it to be, is revealed. It is therefore not scriptual to affirm, as nonetheless the tradition of western Catholic morality has, that procreation is the only ultimate goal of sexuality. (p. 43)

This interrelational dimension of our being is the foundation-stone for a Christian sexual ethic. Maurice Reidy expresses this vividly by saying that 'the design concept' of human sexuality is friendship, not procreation, even though he recognizes that the latter is part of the 'central agenda of human sexuality':

> I strongly suspect that it [friendship] is the ultimate design concept which is embodied in the man and the woman . . . Friendship brings all of the aspects of sexuality into a right alignment with each other, and provides sexuality itself with its reason for being at the heart's core. (*Freedom to Be Friends* (Collins, 1990), pp. 175–6)

Previously the starting-point tended to be the procreational dimension. This led to procreation being viewed as the 'primary end' of marriage. Consequently, over the centuries the Church has developed a *marriage* ethic rather than a sexual ethic based on a sound theology of relationships. This has left single people feeling left out in the cold. It has resulted in a rather negative presentation of Christian celibacy. Moreover, it has relegated childless marriages to the second division and has not been able to offer any positive sexual ethic for homosexual persons. An ethic which interprets human sexuality primarily, though not exclusively, in terms of relationships is more likely to be sufficiently comprehensive to be able to offer positive inspiration to men and women in whatever form of loving commitment they choose to live out their lives.

Although Fuchs's stricture about Western Catholic morality was substantially true in the pre-Vatican II era, things have changed since the Council. *Gaudium et Spes*, while deliberately avoiding the language of primary and secondary ends, puts the relational dimension first in its treatment of marriage. This comes out very clearly in n. 48 which begins the Council's treatment of marriage by a very carefully worded statement of its relational dimension:

> The intimate partnership of married life and love has been established by the Creator and qualified by His laws. It is rooted in the conjugal convenant of irrevocable personal consent. Hence, by that human act whereby spouses mutually bestow and accept each other, a relationship arises which by the divine will and in the eyes of society too is a lasting one.

As is commonly known, the phrase 'mutually bestow and accept *each other*' is a very deliberate alteration of the words of the 1917 Code of Canon Law which spoke of spouses 'mutually bestowing and accepting *the permanent and exclusive right to each other's body with regard to acts which of themselves are apt for bringing about procreation'*.

Likewise, when *Gaudium et Spes* treats of the indissolubility of marriage, once again it puts the interrelational dimension first: 'As a mutual gift of two persons, this intimate union, as well as the good of the children, imposes total fidelity on the spouses and argues for an unbreakable oneness between them' (n. 48).

It would be a misrepresentation of the mind of the Council to suggest that it regards the procreational dimension as an optional extra. There is no doubt that it sees children as one of the intrinsic goods of marriage, a good both for the couple themselves and for the human race to whose continuation they are contributing. Nevertheless, it speaks of children being 'as it were (*veluti*)' the ultimate crown of the couple's love for each other. In other words, the interrelational love of the married couple is good *in itself*. Its goodness is not derivative from their begetting of children. In fact, as Bernard Häring has pointed out in his commentary on this text, 'as it were' is inserted for the precise purpose of qualifying the 'crown' remark in order to emphasize that there is nothing essential lacking in a childless marriage (cf. Herbert Vorgrimler (ed.), *Commentary on the Documents of Vatican II*, V (Burns & Oates/Herder & Herder, 1969), p. 234).

5 Human persons are interdependent social beings

This dimension of being human is self-evident. In our own day the massive growth in the world's population, the increasing availability of international transport and the revolution that has taken place in the communications field have all combined to highlight our essential interdependence. Moreover, it is not merely an interdependence of individual persons. It also applies to the various social groups to which each of us in our various ways belongs. The whole human family is a complex network of interdependent groupings, whether at the level of nations, economic communities, multinational companies, trading partnerships, political affiliations, etc.

This dimension of social interdependence operates dialectically. This aspect of how we operate as human persons has been brought to our attention by the German sociologist Georg Simmel. According to Lewis A. Coser, Simmel saw social interdependence as always involving 'harmony *and* conflict, attraction *and* repulsion, love *and* hatred' (*Masters of Sociological Thought: Ideas in Historical and Social Context* (Harcourt Brace Jovanovich, 1971), p. 184). This was because, in Simmel's view:

> The socialized individual always remains in a dual relation with society:
> he is incorporated within it and yet stands against it. The individual is, at
> the same time, within society and outside it; he exists for society as well
> as for himself: '[Social man] is not partially social and partially individual; rather, his existence is shaped by a fundamental unity, which
> cannot be accounted for in any other way than through the synthesis or
> coincidence of two logically contradictory determinations: man is both
> social link and being for himself, both product of society and life from an

autonomous center.' The individual is determined at the same time as he is determining; he is acted upon at the same time as he is self-actuating. (p. 184)

Simmel is here touching on an aspect of our social interdependence which is often overlooked in theological writing on the community dimension of human life. He argues that a conflict-less human community could not exist empirically. However, this is not a pessimistic stance. According to Coser, Simmel believes in the creative potentiality of conflict:

> Because conflict can strengthen existing bonds or establish new ones, it can be considered a creative, rather than a destructive force. Simmel never dreamed of a frictionless social universe, of a society from which clashes and contentions among individuals and groups would be forever banned. For him, conflict is the very essence of social life, an ineradicable component of social living. The good society is not conflict-free; it is, on the contrary, 'sewn together' by a variety of crisscrossing conflicts among its component parts. (p. 185)

John Paul II seems to interpret the social interdependence in a similar way to Simmel. In a book written prior to becoming pope he speaks of the structures needed for any community or society to be truly human:

> The structure of a human community is correct only if it admits not just the presence of a justified opposition but also that practical effectiveness of opposition required by the common good and the right of participation. (*The Acting Person* (London: Reidel, 1979), p. 287)

The International Theological Commission applied this insight to the relationship between the hierarchical magisterium and theologians:

> The exercise of their functions by the magisterium and by theologians sometimes gives rise to a certain tension. This is not surprising, nor should one expect that such tension can ever be eliminated here on earth. On the contrary, wherever there is authentic life, there will also be some tension. Tension as such is not hostility or real opposition; rather it is a lively stimulus and incentive for both sides to perform their respective tasks in communion with the other, following the method of dialogue. (*Theses on the Relationship between the Ecclesiastical Magisterium and Theology* (1976), pp. 212–13)

What violates this aspect of our social interdependence is not the tension created by conflict or dissent but the voluntary or enforced separation from the community of the person or group who is in conflict with society or its authorities. According to Coser, Simmel would view such a withdrawal from a conflictive relationship as 'wholly negative' (op. cit., p. 185). If this is true, it would put a question mark against the wisdom of some of the actions taken against theologians by the Congregation of the Doctrine of the Faith.

Structures, institutions and laws should not be thought of as a necessary evil we have to endure. They are essential features of our embodiment as applying to the field of social relationships. They are all related to what Catholic social thinkers have termed 'the common good'. This is not something impersonal to which our good as individual persons has to be sacrificed. The common good refers to the state of affairs which is needed in any particular society if the individual goods of its members are to be safeguarded and promoted. Although Vatican II is more concerned about pastoral renewal than precise definitions, it considers the notion of the common good sufficiently important to present a carefully worded definition of it in three different places. For instance, *Gaudium et Spes* follows its treatment of the interdependence of the human person and society with the statement: 'The common good is the sum of those conditions of social life which allow social groups and their individual members relatively thorough and ready access to their own fulfilment' (n. 26; cf. also n. 74 and *Declaration on Religious Freedom*, n. 6).

To say that structures, institutions and laws are indispensable since they flow from this social dimension of being a human person is not to suggest that such structures, institutions and laws are not of human origin. In other words, it is quite consistent with recognizing that they may vary from culture to culture and from age to age. There will always be a changeable dimension to them and, as human constructs, they are necessarily imperfect. That is why it would be a denial of our very humanity to look for some ideal Christian social order. Any political party which claimed to base its manifesto on such an ideal Christian social order is living in a dream-world and is not doing justice to the reality of the human person.

If that is true, what about the body of social thought which goes under the heading of 'Catholic social teaching' and which is clearly so dear to the heart of Pope John Paul II? There is no doubt that sometimes this social thought is spoken of almost as though it is offering some kind of ideal Christian social order. However, a more careful exegesis of the major 'social encyclicals' as seen in their historical context reveals that they were very clearly 'situational' documents. They were responding to particular situations of structural injustice or to dehumanizing social movements which in their day were seriously harming the lives of people, especially the poor. For instance, the very first of the great social encyclicals, *Rerum Novarum* (1891), was a response to some of the problems caused by the Industrial Revolution. Too few people controlled the sources of wealth with the result that very many people were living in dire poverty and enduring inhuman working conditions. *Rerum Novarum* defended the right of workers to form trade unions and demanded a just wage for them. It argued that private property, though a legitimate institution, was only a secondary right and founded on the more basic truth that the goods of this earth are given for the good of all people. It opposed the 'class struggle' as being divisive and so not an effective way of creating a more just society. Hence, it was against the socialist movement of the time because it was so strongly wedded to the 'class struggle'.

A careful exegesis shows that most of the other major social encyclicals have largely followed a similar approach. They attempted to read what seemed to be going on in society in the light of what they saw to be the basic principles for social life which flowed from a Christian world-view. It is this gradual elaboration of these basic principles over the past 100 years that is usually referred to as 'Catholic social teaching'. To a casual observer it can give the impression of offering a blueprint for a Christian social order. When properly understood, it does nothing of the sort. It operates more as a kind of check-list of social values, formulated in various ways, which can be helpful in a critical evaluation of any particular society.

'Catholic social teaching' is often enunciated in the form of general principles which insist on certain facets of social organization that need to be borne in mind if a society is to be truly respectful of human persons. The principle of subsidiarity is a good example of this. It is enunciated in terms of a general principle in *Quadragesimo Anno*, n. 79:

> Just as it is gravely wrong to take from individuals what they can accomplish by their own initiative and industry and give it to the community, so also it is an injustice and at the same time a grave evil and disturbance of right order to assign to a greater and higher association what lesser and subordinate organisations can do.

In fact, this is really a reminder of the dialectical tension existing between the local and central levels in any social organization. In somewhat the same way, the principle stating the limits to private property is a reminder of a similar dialectical tension between the needs of the individual person (or group) and his or her obligations towards the common good. At this level of abstraction these principles make eminently good sense and no person interested in living a wise and loving life would want to question them.

However, real life does not take place on the plane of general principles. As will be explained more fully in Chapter 4, the actual moral 'call' lies in the concrete situation in which the good of human persons is involved. If 'Catholic social teaching', therefore, is really to present the cutting edge of the Gospel, it needs to bring the light of these critical principles to bear on particular situations, using them to evaluate the justice or injustice of what is going on there. Moreover, in the light of that evaluation it needs to challenge those concerned to take the necessary steps to right whatever injustice is being perpetrated.

The form in which 'Catholic social teaching' is presented today recognizes that there are three different levels which have to be considered. These three levels are explained in a document drawn up by the Vatican Congregation for Catholic Education, *Guidelines for the Study and Teaching of the Church's Social Teaching in the Formation of Priests* (30 December 1988). Three distinct levels of the Church's social teaching are identified: (1) 'permanent principles and values'; (2) 'criteria for judgement'; and (3) 'directives for social action'. The first level corresponds to the basic person-centred values which have been the main focus of this chapter. The second level deals more with methodology and involves knowing the reality of the situation (hence, includes social analysis), discerning possible choices and recognizing that new situations demand new judgements. The third level is about process and looks at how we arrive at practical directives for action. Here the focus is on dialogue, participation in solidarity in the struggle for justice, calling on relevant expertise, listening to experience and a basic attitude of openness.

The above tripartite division seems to originate in Paul VI, *Octogesima Adveniens* (1971):

> In the face of such widely varying situations it is difficult for us to utter a unified message and to put forward a solution which has universal validity. Such is not our ambition, nor is it our mission. It is up to the

Christian communities to analyse with objectivity the situation which is proper to their own country, to shed on it the light of the Gospel's unalterable words and to draw principles of reflection, norms of judgment and directives for action from the social teaching of the church. (n. 4)

This same tripartite division is also used by the Congregation for the Doctrine of the Faith in its 1984 *Instruction on Certain Aspects of the 'Theology of Liberation'* (n. 72) and by John Paul II in his 1987 *Sollicitudo Rei Socialis* (n. 41). It certainly seems to have become an accepted element of 'Catholic social teaching'.

This way of understanding 'Catholic social teaching', therefore, seems to acknowledge that if it is to be effective and not merely platitudinous in its generality, it needs to be wedded to a process of dialogue, involving people who are competent to analyse the particular situations being looked at and also involving people who are competent in determining what needs to be done. This is exactly the methodology which the US Bishops' Conference has followed in producing its major pastoral letters, *The Challenge of Peace* (1983) and *Economic Justice for All* (1986). In both instances the bishops held a series of public 'hearings' of experts and those working in the field, and they published two 'draft' versions of each document. Likewise, in his pilgrimages to various countries throughout the world, Pope John Paul II seems to have been at pains to get properly briefed by people familiar with each country and, in some cases at least, has even left the preparation of his addresses substantially in the hands of the local Church.

Naturally, in the field of social justice the end-product of such a process of dialogue need not be a papal encyclical or a pastoral letter of a Bishops' Conference. There is a place for such documents. However, the most important end-product is effective action to remedy the injustice in question. Perhaps this points us to the important truth which is clearly stated in Vatican II but which is even more strongly emphasized by John Paul II in *Christifideles Laici*. In other words, the most appropriate people to bring the Christian world-view to bear on social issues are not the pope or the bishops but lay men and women who are actually involved in the situation. This being so, the priority for those involved in moral teaching in the Church would seem to lie less in issuing public statements and more in helping lay people to draw inspiration and help from 'Catholic social teaching' insofar as it affects their particular field of involvement, be it politics, management, trade unions, communications, medicine or whatever.

6 The human person is a historical being

This means that the human person not only exists in history but also exists *as* history. This is true at all the levels we have looked at already.

As autonomous subjects, our lives are not simply a whole series of disconnected choices. The choices or decisions we make are the very stuff out of which we fashion the person we choose to become. Our so-called 'fundamental option' is not some out-of-history basic decision we make about our lives. It comes into being through the medium of the concrete choices we make in life. Once in being it is further consolidated by subsequent choices in the same direction, or it is weakened by choices inconsistent with it. It can even be radically changed through a choice which either is like the straw that broke the camel's back in terms of this weakening process or else is so deliberately and substantially contradictory to one's fundamental option that it constitutes a moment of 'conversion', whether for good or for evil.

A moral theology organized around the notion of virtues, of character, or of personal story clearly draws much of its strength from this dimension of the human person. These approaches share the common belief that there is more to the moral life than particular choices and decisions. The virtue approach, for instance, has its roots in Aristotle's notion of 'habit'. This recognizes that we gradually become virtuous through repeated acts of virtue. In other words, the virtuous person is the outcome of a long history of acting in this way so that eventually acting virtuously becomes 'second nature' to such a person. Likewise, character needs to be built up. Hence, the emphasis on personal formation and education. Personal story, too, is a continuously unfolding narrative, told in the course of living out our individual lives in history.

Moreover, the historical dimension of being a human person means more than that our lives include a history of free personal choices. Our very capacity to make such choices has its own history of development. Roger Burggraeve has suggested that an awareness of this historical development of our freedom is essential if our moral theology is to have any relevance for the reality of young people's lives:

The ethical feeling, judging, and acting of young people is inevitably marked by the fact that they are 'on the road'. They are at an intermediate phase . . . The adolescent is not yet an ethical adult, but is on the way (perhaps) to becoming such. Especially in our society, in which autonomous responsibility is somehow postponed, this intermediate phase takes a relatively long time. This implies that young persons, in accordance with the psycho-genetic phase through which they are passing, often show a rather tempting and trying, sometimes even provocatively 'deviating' behaviour, marked by a great degree of provisionality . . . We must learn to regard freedom, taking part in the game and learning situation of the period of youth, as that which it is, namely a freedom that has to be explored and conquered by the young person, instead of a mature and balanced freedom one already possesses and controls.

In keeping with this phase of young people's development, what is needed according to Burggraeve is 'an ethics of "passage" or "transition"':

We can also call it an interim ethics or, even stronger, 'growth ethics', in so far as one approaches the period of youth as an interim phase of growth, with the stress on 'growth', without losing sight of what this growth implies for provisionality and the freedom that is not yet completely developed. (All quotations from 'Meaningful living and acting: an ethical and education-pastoral model in Christian perspective', *Louvain Studies* (1988), pp. 152–4)

Likewise, as embodied and interrelational human subjects our lives are obviously historical. Our sexuality, for instance, goes through a staged process of biological development and the hormonal changes accompanying this process have a major impact in the history of our personal maturation. One view of how our sexual orientation comes about suggests that this too is the product, at least partially, of the history of our earliest childhood relationships, especially with our same-sex parent.

As social beings, too, we are essentially historical. We are people of our time and culture. This aspect of the historical dimension of our being is so obvious, it needs no further explanation.

The historical dimension of the human person, like all the other dimensions we have examined, is part of objective reality. Hence, it must not be dismissed on the grounds that it is subjective and irrelevant to 'objective morality'. Objective morality, as has been stressed already, is not about actions divorced from the person doing the action. It is about acting subjects. Chapter 4 will look at the responsibility of acting persons *vis-à-vis* the new possibilities that modern science and technology are opening up in our world today. Accepting our essential historicity implies being prepared to accept the challenge of building the future. Obviously, we have to apply all the human wisdom and experience we have at our disposal to ensure that new developments will not be person-injuring or will not diminish our precious capacity for loving interdependence. Yet we have to be aware that erring on the side of caution may be exactly what it says — erring. And erring means making wrong decisions, which, in the field of morality, means decisions which are dehumanizing and therefore detrimental to wise and loving living. Perhaps, for example, Leo XII thought he was erring on the side of caution when in 1829 he condemned smallpox injections, stating: 'Whoever allows himself to be vaccinated ceases to be a child of God. Smallpox is a judgement of God, the vaccination is a challenge toward heaven' (cf. Louis Janssens, 'Artificial insemination: ethical considerations', *Louvain Studies* (1980), p. 11, n. 12). If the medical world had heeded his warning, enormous suffering world have been allowed to continue needlessly in our world.

7 Human persons are fundamentally equal but each person is unique

Fundamental equality is not claiming that we are all equally gifted, whether in terms of intelligence, or beauty, or temperament, or whatever. Its basis lies in the fact that we are all members of the human species. Human persons are individuals belonging to the species humankind.

Fundamental equality as members of the one species goes hand in hand with uniqueness as individuals within that species. This truth too has very special significance for the human person. This uniqueness contains a degree of originality which is not found in any other species. It links in with the other dimensions of the human person we have already looked at. For instance, as autonomous subjects we are not just individual human clones. We are persons who, in one sense, are self-creating and, in another sense, are the creations of our social, cultural, and familial history. How that combination of influences actually touches each one of us is also unique, as is our personal response to all these factors. Moreover, our originality is increased still further by the web of interpersonal relationships which form the texture of our lives.

Our originality is a very deep dimension of our being a human person. It belongs to that fundamental level at which I can say that I am not just another human person, equal to every other human person. I am Kevin Kelly and, as such, I am absolutely unique — as are you, the reader of this book. We are both originals, just as are all other human persons. Theologically, you and I can say that each of us images God in a way that no other human person ever has or ever will. What a privilege — and what a responsibility!

This dimension of our personal uniqueness raises questions with regard to new possibilities opening out to humankind, especially in the field of genetic therapy and genetic engineering. One of the objections raised against in-vitro fertilization (IVF) is that it would promote an attitude towards children which would regard them as 'products'. This is certainly a possibility in some cases. Whether it is inevitable in all cases is another matter and there is no evidence to show that would be the case. Hence, while it does not constitute a conclusive argument demonstrating the moral unacceptability of IVF, it is a danger that cannot be ignored. Some women theologians have expressed the fear that IVF could lead to a kind of 'quality-control' mentality towards children. This would run counter to that attitude of unconditional welcome and acceptance of a child which is so necessary if the child is to find security in its relationship with its parents. Barbara Katz Rothman fears that we might be surrendering the choice of accepting children as they are. Jean Bethke Elshtain describes aiming for the perfect child as 'human arrogance'. She warns of the devastating effect on parent–child relations when this 'perfect child' turns out, as all children must, to be less than perfect. In fact, the very concept of a 'perfect child' smacks more of a consumer product for the market and would seem to be in contradiction to personal uniqueness.

Nevertheless, it cannot be denied that parents have always tried to influence the human 'quality' of their children. The whole nurturing and educational process is directed towards 'forming' their children — and this includes religious up-bringing as well. Hence, in a sense it is very natural and very good for parents to want the best for their children. However, there is a very delicate line between 'wanting the best' and 'determining the best'. Because their children are human persons in their own right, the 'best' would seem to include safeguarding and even increasing their children's capacity for self-determination. There is a subtle but crucial difference between education and manipulation. Education is to do with empowering a child to achieve self-determination. Manipulation is a dominative exercise of power by parents over their children aimed, albeit unconsciously perhaps, at determining their children's identity as persons.

If the diminution of the capacity for self-determination is seen as a violation of a person's dignity in the social and educational field, the same must surely be true with regard to modifications in a person's make-up that it might be possible to bring about through genetic therapy and engineering. Truly human therapy is directed towards enabling a person to live as fully as possible as an individual member of humankind. Hence, it seeks to cure or even eliminate pathological factors which diminish a person's options in life. However, if genetic therapy were used to exaggerate certain human traits (e.g. tallness for athletic or sporting prowess, intelligence through 'Nobel Prize quality' breeding, etc.), the likely outcome would be that a person would be to that extent 'distanced' from his or her fellow human beings. That would surely have a major impact on determining such a person's 'originality'. To that extent his or her uniqueness as a person would be deliberately determined by other people. I suggest that that would constitute a violation of a most sacred dimension of our being a human person. The same kind of consideration would put a large question mark against parents choosing the sex of their children, if genetic engineering ever made this a possibility for humans.

8 The human person is called to know and worship God

Janssens lists this among the essential dimensions of being a human person. At first sight it seems the odd one out on the list and it is noticeable that Janssens gives it a much briefer treatment than the other dimensions. I was almost inclined to omit it from the list altogether since it seemed to operate on a completely different plane. However, the more I thought about it, the more I realized that it was crucial. Without it our attempt to delineate the major dimensions of being a human person would be fundamentally flawed. To omit this dimension would be to give a seriously incomplete account of the human person. Such an account, therefore, would not correspond to reality as we know it.

I would interpret the 'know and worship God' dimension of being a human person as being a way of expressing the openness of the human person to the experience of transcendence. This refers to our capacity to be lost in wonder before the mystery of reality. It is that dimension of us that is able to register 'mystery' and not just 'puzzlement' in face of those experiences in life which go beyond the limits of our human comprehension. The roots of this dimension do not lie in our ignorance, the fact that we encounter certain phenomena whose causes we cannot determine for the present. Its roots lie not in our ignorance but in the wealth of our understanding. It is almost as though the more we come to understand reality, the more we are led to be lost in wonder before it. It is recognizing that, although our 'eye' can see something quite clearly, there is nevertheless more to it than meets the eye. It is this sense of wonder which seeks expression through such adjectives as 'wonder-ful', 'mind-blowing', etc. Hugh Lavery refers to this dimension as the 'really real'. Gerard Manley Hopkins speaks of 'the beauty, deep down things'.

One of the most comprehensive articulations of this transcendent dimension of being a human person is given by David Tracy is his book *Plurality and Ambiguity* (SCM, 1987). It is worth quoting at length:

> Any human being can ask the fundamental questions that are part of the very attempt to become human at all . . . religious or limit questions: questions provoked by radical contingency and mortality; questions evoked by the transience of all things human; questions attendant upon an acknowledgement of the historical and social contingency of all the values embraced and all the convictions lived by; the question of suffering, that contrast experience par excellence, which enters every life at some point to interrupt its continuities and challenge its seeming security; . . . the question of why we sense some responsibility to live an ethical life even when we cannot rationally prove why we should be ethical at all; the question why we might need to affirm a belief that there is some fundamental order in reality that allows scientific enquiry; the question of the possible nature of that order revealed in the new physics and the new astronomies and cosmologies; the question of how to understand the oppression endured by so many of the living as well as the subversive memories of the suffering of the dead alive in the narratives, sagas, and folktales of every people; . . . the question of the need to understand what possible meaning might be present in the profound love and joy we experience; the question of why I possess a fundamental trust that both allows me to go on at all and is reducible to all my other trusts; the question of why an occasional sense, however transient, of the sheer giftedness of reality can be experienced when I finally stop clinging and sense the truth in Wittgenstein's

statement 'That the world is, is the mystical'; the question of whether
I too experience moments that bear some family resemblance to
those 'consolations without a cause' of which the mystics wrote . . .
(pp. 86–7)

As Tracy suggests, this crucial dimension of being human is not
only compatible with the scientific mind. It actually undergirds the
scientific mind and finds expression in the very practice of science.
Asked in a 1990 television interview whether some areas of life
should not be 'no go' areas for scientists, a US genetic biologist,
Dr Marilyn Singer, replied that her research into the human genome
inspired her with a greater, not a lesser, sense of reverence for life.
Almost mystically she asserted that since we meet the wonder of life
in the whole of reality, why should we reject the privilege of discovering even more amazing indications of this wonder. The 'scientific mentality' is sometimes equated with an anti-religious attitude
to life. Contrary to that, I would suggest that scientists who are
truly committed to science may well be the people today who have
a very privileged experience of wonder. After all, as Dr Singer
commented, they are the 'explorers' of today, going where human
beings have never been before.

I concluded an earlier book which studied the responses of the
various Christian Churches to IVF with a comment which might
bear repeating in the present context:

> Reverence for life is an attitude of wonder before the ultimate mystery
> of life . . . Does the intrusion of scientific technology and research
> into the reproductive process destroy this sense of wonder or can it
> provoke wonder in a new way? . . . Do science and technology cause
> reverence to be eroded in the human heart or can they actually pro-
> vide the opportunity for an entirely new human experience of rever-
> ence? . . .
>
> If the Christian churches claim some expertise in the field of 'rever-
> ence', they have to face some challenging questions on this point. For
> instance, does reverence demand an attitude of non-interference with
> the basic natural processes of life and love — 'Come no nearer. Take off
> your shoes, for the place on which you stand is holy ground' (Ex 3.5)?
> Or does reverence also embrace a practical attitude of bringing relief to
> couples by employing scientific technology to help them have children
> when their natural reproductive faculties are found to be defective — 'Is
> it against the law on the sabbath to do good, or to do evil; to save life, or
> to destroy it?' (Lk 6.9) Or can reverence even take the form of believing
> that God has empowered humankind to work 'even greater wonders'
> (cf. Jn 14.12) than are found in creation itself? In other words, does

reverence allow, and perhaps even require, humankind to alter and improve on the natural processes of reproduction, if this is considered to be humanly beneficial? (*Life and Love* (Collins, 1987), p. 153)

Tracy mentions basic ethical concerns among the fundamental life questions. Gabriel Daly is obviously thinking along the same lines when he writes:

Tyrrell, who once wrote that 'morality divorced from mysticism is a lean sort of religion', believed that conscience properly understood is far more than a 'merely moral or ethical experience'; it is also 'a religious and mystical experience'. That, in my view, is the true meaning of the statement that conscience is the voice of God. (In Seán Freyne (ed.), *Ethics and the Christian* (Dublin: Columba, 1991), pp. 73–4)

In a similar way Vatican II locates the deepest operation of conscience within this dimension of the human person: 'Conscience is the most secret core and sanctuary of a person. There one is alone with God, whose voice echoes in one's depths' (*Gaudium et Spes*, n. 16). Something similar could be said of the Ignatian emphasis on 'the discernment of spirits'.

Of course, this dimension of transcendence is not limited to our response to what one might call the 'magnificent' realities encountered in life. It is a level of appreciation which covers the whole of our experience of life, even though it might perhaps be 'felt' more keenly in some situations than in others. It is certainly not restricted to what is sometimes called 'religious experience'. In fact, some instances of so-called 'religious experience' may be traced back to roots which are quite alien to this transcendent dimension in us. On the other hand, a person's capacity to see 'deep down things' often seems to be active in a special way in 'crisis' or 'limit' experiences in life. It is almost as though the crisis experience of disintegration followed by reintegration puts a person in touch with a deeper level of his or her being.

Rosemary Haughton offers a striking example of this in her article 'Marriage in women's new consciousness', in William P. Roberts (ed.), *Commitment to Partnership* (Mahwah, NJ: Paulist Press, 1987). Speaking of her experience with young women struggling to repair shattered lives, she writes:

For many women, the moment of conversion, the true metanoia, has come when they reach the decision to seek a divorce . . . To compare the decision to seek a divorce to the choice of discipleship may seem shocking — but that can be what it really is: the choice of life over death, spiritual freedom over bondage. It is for many the entrance into a new life. (pp. 149-50)

The same process can be seen at work in the way physical suffering, evil though it is, can sometimes occasion personal growth at a very deep level. Margaret Spufford was persuaded to write an account of how this was true in her own life of pain and suffering which she does not hesitate to describe as 'an unmitigated evil'. Yet very significantly her book is entitled *Celebration* (Collins, 1989). She describes very powerfully how this transcendental dimension can be operative even in the midst of almost unbearable suffering: 'I think I can say, without any trace of masochism, that the disease has indeed been a creative medium. I have tried to use the pain of it to remind me to try to focus on what is really important. And what is really important is adoration' (p. 93).

Schillebeeckx, in his book *Jesus in Our Western Culture: Mysticism in Ethics and Politics* (SCM, 1987), maintains that this transcendental dimension is also at work in the field of what Jon Sobrino would call 'political holiness'. For Schillebeeckx the 'contrast experience' of human dignity being violated and the emotion this arouses in us can be the medium of a deep encounter with God's action in human life. For the person being oppressed this is a kind of negative experience of transcendence since such a person 'experiences that God is absent from many human relationships of possession and power in this world; thus he or she experiences the alienation, the gap, between God, the Kingdom of God and our society'. The believer who stands genuinely in solidarity with the oppressed 'experiences precisely in his or her political love and opposition to injustice an intense contact with God, the presence of the liberating God of Jesus . . . In this, awareness grows that God reveals himself as the deepest mystery, the heart and soul of any truly human liberation' (p. 73). Schillebeeckx does not hesitate to describe both these experiences as 'mystical'.

Writing of this dimension of being human Tracy comments: 'Religious questions deliberately ask the question of the meaning and truth of Ultimate Reality not only as it is in itself but as it is existentially related to us' (p. 87). This raises the whole question of revelation, the possibility of a special self-disclosure of this 'Ultimate Reality' to human beings. Christianity believes that such a self-disclosure has actually taken place in the history of a particular people and most uniquely in the person of Jesus Christ. The impact of this self-disclosure on the human enterprise of wise and loving living is examined in Chapter 6. This chapter is left until late in the book since it presupposes the practice of wise and loving living — 'The unlived life is not worth reflecting upon'. Its purpose is to delve into the deeper meaning of wise and loving living — 'The unreflective life is not worth living'. (I am grateful to Tracy for the complementary contrasting of these two classic Buddhist and Socratic sayings.)

Chapter 4

IN THE LIGHT OF EXPERIENCE:
MORALITY AND CHANGE

Change is an important part of being truly human. Hence, we must recognize that a truly human morality demands change. Moreover, a Christian should be in the forefront of those acknowledging that morality of its very essence implies change. Christianity believes in God's call to conversion. And conversion necessitates change. It is about discovering for today what sort of conversion is needed on the part of both individuals and society as a whole. We will only come to know what kind of change is demanded of us through an honest analysis of the inhumanities of modern-day life and where their root causes lie, whether in personal attitudes or in institutional structures or, as is most likely, in an interaction of both. Moreover, such an honest analysis means that we ourselves must change. It implies a willingness to open our eyes and be converted from our blindness to the inhumanities existing around us and in which we ourselves are probably colluding in some way or other. Furthermore, as we have already seen in Chapter 1, the Church itself is not exempt from this need for conversion. That demands an honest look at the way the Church is being called to change in our day.

To acknowledge that the Church is constantly called to change immediately raises the question: Can the Church's moral teaching change? What should we think about the possibility of admitting that what we formerly believed to be morally right might be wrong, or vice versa? Would this destroy the credibility of all the moral truths we believe? Would it create a crisis of confidence among Catholics in the teaching authority of the Church? I do not believe it would. After all, the very nature of our moral knowledge is such that we should expect it to develop and at times be modified or even corrected, as we grow in understanding of ourselves as human beings and of the world to which we belong. Our human experience plays an essential role in our coming to understand what at a practical level furthers the promotion of our basic human goods in everyday life. For instance, it is through experience that we come to see what kind of life-style promotes or injures the basic good of human health. It is through experience that we discover what kind of family relating best promotes children's growth to maturity. The same experience also reveals the other side of the coin to us, how family dysfunctioning can cause havoc in relationships of later life.

To recognize that our moral knowledge is susceptible to growth, change and even correction should make us humble, yet confident, as we face the challenging decisions of our day which are likely to open up entirely new possibilities for future generations. Humility should come from the recognition that future generations may need to modify or correct some decisions we make today. Confidence should flow from the recognition that we are called to continue the tradition of our forebears who had the courage in their day to make decisions which, despite all their ambiguity, have opened up what to them was the future but which to us is the present.

The process of change will not be properly tackled if we give in to the temptation always to be looking for absolute certainties. Human decision-making is not like that. It involves balancing the different values at play in a situation, assessing various possibilities and probabilities, being prepared to take prudent risks.

What is unchangeable: our foundational belief in the dignity of the human person

Nevertheless, it would be misleading to give the impression that we are floundering around hopelessly in an inescapable moral morass. There are basic values on which we take our stand with absolute conviction. Standing by these values represents what Havel has termed 'living in the truth'. Admittedly we can meet situations of moral dilemma in which a variety of values we believe in are involved and we do not seem to be able to do full justice to them all. Nevertheless, even in those situations, to adopt some kind of compromise solution need not imply that we are rejecting the value which we have decided has to take second place in this instance. All that has happened is that we have judged that the other values at stake are of greater importance or at least are involved in this situation in a much more substantial way. As we saw in Chapter 3, at the heart of our Christian and human value system lies our belief in the dignity of the human person. Were that foundational principle to be abandoned, of course, we would no longer be dealing with a phenomenon that could be called human morality in the proper sense of the word.

What cannot change in human morality, therefore, is our foundational belief in the dignity of the human person. This is why certain forms of behaviour are recognized as so completely in violation of this dignity that they are described as 'crimes against humanity'. Sadly the overthrow of the Nazi regime has not heralded the eradication of such crimes from the face of the earth. The advance of civilization in the twentieth century seems to have brought with it new possibilities for even more abominable crimes against humanity. It is significant that Vatican II, although it deliberately tried to avoid issuing condemnations, felt the need to put flesh and blood on its presentation of reverence for the human person in *Gaudium et Spes*. As we saw in Chapter 2, it rounded off its treatment of this topic in n. 27 with an extensive catalogue of inhuman actions which offend against reverence for the human person.

The philosopher Anthony Kenny maintains that we could not have a common human morality without some kind of statement or code excluding certain forms of behaviour as fundamentally in violation of the basic values the human community subscribes to. He views such a universally applicable code as one of the elements 'constitutive of morality' itself. For him it is an essential part of 'the belief that any member of any moral community belongs to the single community which is the human race'. This means that 'there are moral relationships, and shared values and codes, between any two human beings' (Anthony Kenny, 'Abortion and the taking of human life' in Peter Byrne (ed.), *Medicine in Contemporary Society* (King's College Studies, 1986–87), p. 89).

If we acknowledge the social dimension of all human action, based on our essential interdependence, it would be accurate to describe every wrong action as a crime against humanity. However, common usage understandably tends to restrict this term to actions which blatantly and massively violate the basic humanity of some of our fellow human beings. Since we share a common humanity, a major violation of the humanity of one human person is seen as an attack on the dignity of the whole human family. We all feel violated and it is only natural that we should experience a deep sense of anger at such a violation.

This surely is why the whole issue of abortion, and most recently embryo research, is such an emotive issue. As we shall see in Chapter 5, women theologians particularly, though not exclusively, are making us face up to the importance of feelings in our lives, especially the feeling of anger when we are faced with a violation of human dignity. People who genuinely believe that from the moment of fertilization what we are dealing with is a human being with the full dignity of a human person will understandably *feel* deeply about abortion and embryo research, since in their eyes this is a blatant and massive violation of the dignity of some of our fellow human beings. For them this really does deserve to be described as a crime against humanity. It is something which should provoke deep feelings of anger. Seen from that angle, it is perfectly understandable that emotions should run high. If they did not, they could rightly be criticized as being disembodied in their moral stance.

However, this holds equally on the other side too, especially with women who are deeply committed to the 'pro-choice' position. They would see the dehumanization of women by the patriarchal stranglehold over society, culture and religion throughout most of human history as a crime against humanity. This crime can only be redeemed by the liberation of women and a crucial component of that liberation is the full acceptance of the moral agency of women in theory and in practice. Moreover, in the eyes of these women a major area where that moral agency needs to be recognized lies in women's responsibility for their own bodies, including their reproductive potential and any actuation of this potential in pregnancy. The women who argue this position most cogently insist that this is not a pro-abortion stance as such. They recognize that for a woman to choose to have an abortion is a very serious moral decision (cf. my earlier book *Life and Love*, p. 92). What they are insisting on, however, is that that decision, however serious, is ultimately the decision of the woman. For the law to deny women this right, they say, is to perpetuate the structural dehumanization of women. Hence they see this issue as having major symbolic value in liberating women from the crime against humanity which has been perpetrated against them for most of history. So here, too, someone convinced of this position will *feel* very deeply about it. Anger is very appropriate and so emotions are bound to run high on this issue also.

Human morality must reject what it sees to be crimes against humanity. The point at issue in the heated debate about embryo research and abortion is not whether we can change our morality and believe that what is acknowledged to be a crime against humanity can be morally acceptable. That is impossible as it would destroy the whole basis of our morality. Both sides in the above debate do not disagree about the need to oppose crimes against humanity.

They disagree on whether this particular action (destructive embryo research or abortion) is *de facto* a crime against humanity. Since the issue is one of such importance, it is crucial that both sides in this disagreement really try to engage each other in dialogue. Because of the strong feelings involved, such dialogue is not easy. In my previous book *Life and Love* (Collins, 1987, pp. 140–4) I summarized and commented on two sets of guide-lines offered for this dialogue by Richard McCormick and Daniel Callahan. I believe they still have much to offer.

Deciding the future

What about all the possibilities for change in the way we live our lives which science and technology are beginning to offer humanity this century? After all, embryo research is merely one of many completely new possibilities that modern science is opening up to humankind. In-vitro fertilization is already with us, gene therapy and even human genetic engineering are just round the corner. Major advances in the field of communications technology are beginning to effect major changes in our life-style. Hence, we need to take a close look at our moral beliefs and the new ways of envisaging reality that modern science is opening out to us.

Yearning for a past golden age that never actually existed will get us nowhere. Neither will a naive belief that every change is a change for the better and must be accepted uncritically as human progress. Avoiding both those extremes, we need to look at how we can most responsibly approach the future. What precise ethical principles do we need to forge for ourselves in order to ensure that the true dignity of human persons will be best served as we wrestle with decisions which will profoundly affect the lives of future generations of human persons? There is a growing conviction among many people that we have violated nature without properly understanding the intrinsic interdependence of all its parts and that now we are beginning to pay the cost.

Does that imply that we would now be wise to adopt a kind of 'nature knows best' ethical principle? Or would that simply be evading our responsibility as the only fully conscious and rational beings on the planet? Could it even be argued that we have a God-given mandate to 'improve on' nature? Should we set out sights on trying to arrive at some kind of universal, world-wide morality?

Or do we need to accept that there will always be a variety of moral beliefs and practices since, as we saw in Chapter 3, human beings are essentially historical and cultural creatures? If we are going to be able to wrestle with these issues, we need to look more closely at how we come to arrive at and formulate our moral knowledge. This will help us explore how we can provide ourselves with a moral theology which will be of help to us as we face up to major decisions which will determine the future of humankind.

The relevance of human experience for moral knowledge

Increasingly today theologians are insisting that human experience is an indispensable and fundamental source for developing our moral knowledge. Cardinal Hume made this point at the 1983 Rome Synod on the Family:

> The prophetic mission of . . . husbands and wives is based upon their experience as married persons and on an understanding of the sacrament of marriage of which they can speak with their own authority. This experience and this understanding constitute, I would suggest, an authentic source of theology from which we, the pastors, and indeed the whole Church can draw.

The point has often been made that etymologically our word 'expert' comes from the word 'experience'. An expert is a person who has learned from experience. The validity of that observation is being acknowledged more and more in our own day. People tend to be suspicious of what they call 'book learning'. So-called 'experts' have so often been proved wrong by the way things turned out. Experience has called their bluff, as it were. Jack Mahoney comments that it is experience which leads to people being acknowledged as authorities in their field. As he says, the authority of experience has no need to demand a hearing. It naturally commands a hearing.

To a large extent, our ethical principles are no more than generalizations which humanity has gradually arrived at through the lived experience of wise and loving persons. Probably often by dint of trial and error, they have discovered for their time and for their particular circumstances what ways of individual and communal living and relating best serve their well-being as human persons and answer their deepest needs. In a sense, our moral principles are the product of a host of conscience-decisions made by our forebears. These conscience-decisions have led them eventually to formulate the most important fruits of their experience in some sort of moral code or system of taboos. A recent writer, commenting on the parallel between the acquisition of scientific knowledge and the acquisition of moral knowledge, even went so far as to describe conscience as 'the laboratory of ethics' (Manuel García Doncel, 'Historical epistemology and the evolution of ethics' in *Human Life: Its Beginnings and Development: Bioethical Reflections by Catholic Scholars* (International Federation of Catholic Universities, 1988), p. 254). In other words, to a large extent our ethical knowledge is drawn from human experience and consequently needs to be reassessed in the light of further experience. William James even went so far as to say: 'There is no such thing as an ethical philosophy dogmatically made up in advance . . . There can be no final truth in ethics any more than in physics, until the last man [and woman — *my insertion*] has had his experience and said his say' (quoted by Albert R. Jonsen and Stephen Toulmin, *The Abuse of Casuistry* (University of California, 1988), p. 282).

Jack Mahoney is critical of the tendency to view moral reasoning simply as the application of moral principles to particular situations. That does not allow the situation to influence the principle and 'does not give sufficient consideration to the origin of moral principles themselves' ('Moral reasoning in medical ethics', *The Month* (September, 1985), p. 293). These moral principles represent the collective wisdom of humankind, being 'the cumulative common element in a succession of significantly similar situations'. This leads Mahoney to write:

It follows from this that moral principles are made for situations, and not situations for moral principles . . . Moreover, really new situations challenge established moral principles to give an account of themselves . . . in terms of the underlying reasoning which gives rise to such principles. In other words, . . . there is a continual dialectical process between principles and situations, between facts and moral reflection, a two-way traffic rather than simply a one-way application of principles. In identifying a discrepancy between the situation as it really is and the situation as it is described (and *ipso facto* evaluated), not only is it established that this situation does not 'come under' the moral principle in mind, but the moral principle itself is subjected to scrutiny and refinement . . . In one sense all this can be summed up in the old adage that 'circumstances alter cases', but there is more to it than that . . . circumstances also alter principles. (Ibid., p. 294)

This ties in with a recognition that human decision-making should be a creative process. It is not like painting by numbers, obeying the instructions of the artist who has already decided what the picture is going to be. In an article in *The Way* I expressed the same point through slightly different metaphors:

> In a sense we create God's will; or better, God's will takes shape through our decisions. We are not puppets with the whole of our lives and everything we do already pre-programmed by God, the puppet-master. As each major decision looms before us in life, God's will is not already determined and filed away in some kind of divine computer programme. Discovering God's will is not a matter of discovering what God has already decided that we should do. Rather, discovering God's will lies in ourselves deciding what is the most loving and responsible thing for us to do. We discover God's will by actually bringing it into being. ('Towards an adult conscience', *The Way* (1985), p. 286)

This is not to reject moral principles or fall into the error of situation ethics. Although moral principles help to make us aware of the human values that need to be respected in various situations or ways of acting, we need more than these principles if we are to do justice to the demands of human situations in all their particularity. Schillebeeckx insists that particular situations themselves contain within them the needs of persons to which some sort of response is called for. It is as if the voice of God was calling from the midst of this situation:

> Only and exclusively as intrinsically individualized is 'being human' a reality and can it be the source of moral norms (which in religious parlance, we can rightly describe as the will of God). Therefore, there is only one source of ethical norms, namely, the historical reality of the value of the inviolable human person with all its bodily and social implications. That is why we cannot attribute validity to abstract norms as such. Moreover, no abstract statement can produce a call or invitation . . . Therefore, these abstract, generally valid norms are an inadequate yet real *pointer* to the one real, concrete ethical norm, namely, this concrete human person living historically in this concrete society. (*God the Future of Man* (Sheed & Ward, 1969), p. 151)

The Good Samaritan did not see the wounded traveller as an instance of the universal principle to love one's neighbour as oneself. He was moved to action by pity for this poor man's plight and not by any abstract principle. This is the mind-set found in most of the moral utterances of the Old Testament prophets. They are not enunciating moral principles as such. They are exposing unwise and unloving living on the part of God's people — and in this way they are also 'revealing' what needs to be done.

This is why conscience formation is just as much about the development of human sensitivity as it is about being educated in the principles of morality. In his book *The Christian of the Future* (Burns and Oates, 1966), Karl Rahner wrote that Christians today need 'an absolute conviction that the moral responsibility of the individual is not at an end because he does not come into conflict with any concrete instruction of the official Church'. He went on to say that what individual Christians needed from the Church was 'an initiation into the holy art of finding the concrete prescription for his own decision in the personal call of God'. He described this as 'the logic of concrete particular decision which of course does justice to universal regulative principles but cannot wholly be deduced from them solely by explicit casuistry' (all quotations from pp. 46–7).

It is also important to recognize that in the light of experience some of our principles may need to be revised in order to do justice to our deeper understanding of ourselves and our world. This has implications for the moral teaching of the Church. If the Church fails to listen to the experience of good-living people within and outside the Christian community, it is failing in its task as a moral teacher. In the report he published as a result of his six listening sessions with women on abortion Archbishop Weakland has pointed out: 'listening is an important part of any teaching process; the church's need to listen is no exception' ('Listening sessions on abortion: a response', *Origins* (31 May 1990), p. 35).

The development of moral knowledge and understanding is clearly very important. It is in fact nothing less than a deepening of our grasp of God's call to us to be as fully human as possible in the world in which we live. By the same token we should recognize the importance of being open to revising our moral understanding in the light of new human experience. New moral insights can enrich our whole outlook on life and more adequately formulated moral principles can serve as direction markers to guide us along the new paths we have to take as we continue the journey undertaken so wisely and lovingly by those who have gone before us.

Natural law and experience

It is easy to say that we should be open to revising our moral understanding in the light of experience. It is more difficult to spell out
exactly what is meant by learning from experience in the field of
morality. In what precise sense do we learn from experience?

Obviously, to the extent that our experimental knowledge about
ourselves as human beings increases we arrive at a better understanding of how we function as physical, biological, sexual,
emotional, psychological and social beings. However, does this
understanding of how we 'function' as human beings tell us immediately how we 'ought' to live? Some people would claim that it
does. They would say that this experimental knowledge about ourselves reveals to us the 'Maker's instructions'. A good life consists in
living in conformity with these instructions. Some have interpreted
the 'natural law' in this way. We obey the natural law, they would
say, by living in conformity with our nature — and by 'nature' they
mean how human beings 'function' naturally. Hence they then proceed to condemn certain ways of acting as 'unnatural' or contrary to
the natural law.

For them nature is thought of in terms of 'givenness'. We receive
ourselves as 'given' from God. As such our nature has to be
respected. It must not be interfered with in any way. To interfere
with nature is to 'play God'. It is to invade a 'no go' area which is
forbidden territory for us.

This way of viewing 'nature' is foreign to the way we tend to see
things nowadays. For one thing, we now know that what we call our
'nature' is the result of historical evolution over billions of years. In
other words, if we are to speak of the 'givenness' of human nature we
must include its historicity as part of its givenness. What is 'given'
can too easily be interpreted as what is static and unchangeable. The
only human nature that exists and that is 'given' to us is our human
nature which we experience at this point in its history and our history. To make human nature something static would, in fact, be to
interfere with it since our nature is essentially historical. If we are to
respect human nature as 'given', we must respect it as historical.

Another problem with the 'givenness' approach I have been questioning is that it does not do justice to the truth that the nature we
share is that of human persons. In fact, the most fundamental
dimension of ourselves that we share in common with each other is
precisely that dimension which makes us uniquely different from

each other, namely the fact that as persons we are subjects with intelligence and free will, charged with responsibility for our own destiny. However, as we saw at great length in Chapter 3, that dimension must not be isolated from the other dimensions of our nature as human persons. Though unique persons, we are essentially embodied, interdependent and social beings whose destiny is bound up with the history of the rest of material creation. The whole of creation, and the human family in a very special way, is 'gifted' by God. Because of our special 'giftedness' as human persons we have to use our God-given gifts intelligently — which means wisely and lovingly. Perhaps 'gifted' expresses the truth more adequately than 'given'.

With the understanding we now have we can see that history is not simply something that we stand back from and view as intelligent observers. It is something that we actually participate in. With our modern consciousness of this historical dimension of ourselves and our world we are now able to appreciate in a way unknown to our forebears that in the long process of learning from experience over the centuries they were actually playing their part in 'forming' the human nature that we have inherited from them. What they did unconsciously we are able to do much more consciously. As mentioned above, they no doubt learned from their mistakes. Today, with the advance of modern technology, in many areas of life we cannot afford the luxury of learning from our mistakes. The stakes are too high. We are now capable of mistakes that could wipe out the human race and destroy all life on our planet.

Yet precisely because the stakes are so high we have to be at our most intelligent. Humankind today has to face problems concerning human life and well-being which would have been unthinkable to previous generations. The problem of world population has never had to be faced before. An approach based on a static view of 'givenness' has no solution to offer to this problem. Never before have the nations of the world been so completely interdependent as they are at this point in history. The need for some kind of international peace-keeping body is making us look more closely at the role of the United Nations. We are becoming more aware that the manipulation of the United Nations (or any other international forum, the GATT talks, for instance) in order to serve the self-interest of one nation or a group of nations regardless of the harm done to others is tantamount to a crime against humanity.

Far-seeing people with a world-vision are noting that what is most endangering peace throughout the world is not the aggression of individual nations. Rather it is a system of trade and finance throughout the world in which the chips are heavily stacked in favour of the major transnational corporations and their (mainly Western) beneficiaries. In the long run this is threatening the well-being and stability of our whole planet. A static 'givenness' approach is powerless to offer any solution to such an enormous problem. Such a 'givenness' approach divorces private property from social responsibility and gives it a 'stability' which is foreign to the older and more venerable tradition in the Church. That tradition teaches that the goods of this earth are 'gifts' from God to be used for the benefit of all. Pope Paul VI reminded us of this tradition by quoting the words of St Ambrose:

> You are not making a gift of your possessions to the poor person. You are handing over to him what is his. For what has been given in common for the use of all, you have arrogated to yourself. The world is given to all, and not only to the rich. (*Populorum Progressio* (1967), n. 23)

Catholic social teaching on private property refuses to absolutize the *status quo*. The foundational truth on which the institution of private property is based is not the unfettered freedom and privacy of independent and totally autonomous individuals, giving them the right to use their possessions in any way they please, regardless of the needs of others. It lies more particularly in a subtle combination of the various dimensions of being a human person, particularly the dimensions of 'subject', 'embodied', 'interdependent' and 'unique'. Private property is a kind of extension of our freedom as personal subject into the material world, enabling us to interrelate socially to other persons and also giving us scope to exercise and develop our personal uniqueness. However, this delicate balance of the various dimensions is destroyed if one dimension is emphasized to the exclusion or detriment of the others.

The revolutionary challenge of this 'giftedness' of private property is relevant to the question of the crippling debt of many Third World countries. The enormity of their debts to First World banks and its killing (literally) effects on the poor in their countries is beginning to make people raise ethical questions about the way interest and debt operate in the financial world of today. It seems that the fundamental starting-point from which our present stance on lending and interest developed was the paradigm case that it is wrong to demand interest on a loan to a person in dire need (cf. Albert R. Jonsen and Stephen Toulmin, *The Abuse of Casuistry* (1988), p. 191). Perhaps we have left the challenge of that starting-point too far behind.

There is another strand to modern-day thinking which could be called the 'ecological mind' and this has a strong belief in the good-ness of whatever is 'natural'. Could not the static 'givenness' view claim to have the support of the 'modern mind' in this sense? There is no doubt that the 'ecological mind' recognizes a basic 'goodness' in what we are accustomed to call 'nature'. For instance, the 'ecological mind' believes in a basic simplicity of life-style and promotes such things as 'natural foods' and 'organic farming'. For some it would also include the practice of 'natural family planning' since this is based on respect for the 'natural processes' of our human nature in its physical/biological dimension. What are we to make of this? Is their belief that 'nature' should be respected in direct contradiction to what I have been arguing above?

If it took the form of a 'back-to-nature' campaign which rejected all the achievements of modern science and technology, it would certainly be in contradiction to what I have been saying. However, I do not believe that such an extreme position is a true representative of the 'ecological mind' as found today, especially in many young people. What I hear from the 'ecological mind' today is a timely warning. It recognizes the enormous power and influence of modern technology and it is warning us to keep technology in its place. Technology operates at the level of means, not ends. It is meant to serve us and help us in our search for human well-being. However, such are the wonders of modern technology, we can easily be seduced by its achievements and be caught up in the frenzied rush to develop more and more advanced technology. Faced with yet another development in modern technology, the 'ecological mind' puts two vital questions to the 'technological mind': (1) What is this new piece of technology for? Is it really promoting human well-being in the fullest sense of the world? and (2) What about its long-term consequences and its accidental side-effects? Are these being sufficiently taken into account?

In a sense, the 'ecological mind' is keeping the issue of 'due propor-tion' on the agenda. It is very conscious, perhaps at times over-conscious, of the ambiguity of modern progress and technology. It keeps asking: Is it worth it? In other words, is the good being achieved in proportion to the damage or harm that might be the cost of achieving this good? Moreover, the 'ecological mind' tends to have a global vision. And a global vision cannot but be struck by the extremes of prosperity and poverty which coexist on our planet and which are a disgrace to our race. Hence, the 'ecological mind' starts asking other questions at the level of 'ends'. How authentically 'human' is the concentration of human ingenuity, wealth and effort on the advancement of technology when the same resources could be employed to alleviate the problem of poverty in our world and to tackle its root causes? Are there any hidden agendas at work in all this? It is interesting to note that these are similar to some of the basic questions posed by the US bishops in their 1986 Pastoral Letter *Economic Justice for All*. Using their impact on the poor as the yard-stick for the authentic humanity of any economic (or technological) measures, they posed three probing questions:

> Decisions must be judged in the light of what they do *for* the poor, what they do *to* the poor and what they enable the poor to do *for* themselves. The fundamental moral criterion for all economic decisions, policies and institutions is this: They must be at the service of *all people, especially the poor*. (n. 24)

The 'ecological mind' is an important dimension of good human common sense. It stands at the other side of the spectrum to the 'technological mind' but this might be no bad thing. Perhaps through a dialectic of creative tension both need to make their own specific contribution to the common search for authentic human living in today's world. If this is true, they both have their role to play in helping the human family achieve what is in accord with the natural law in today's world. They both highlight concerns that must be taken into account by human intelligence, if in today's world it is to 'reason rightly', as Aquinas would say.

The emphasis of the 'ecological mind' is on the natural 'function-ing' of things — how created reality as a whole functions and how we human beings, as participating parts of this creative reality, function. That the human family increases its understanding and appreciation of this dimension is of crucial importance for life, human and non-human, on our planet. However, though this knowledge is very significant from an ethical point of view, in itself it does not provide us with an ethical norm for action. Philosophi-cally, the natural law does not consist in 'nature' nor even in our knowledge of 'nature'. It consists in our appropriation of this knowledge and our making use of it in trying to discern what kind of personal and social living is most conducive to the safeguarding and promotion of the dignity of human persons. Josef Fuchs puts this in theological language when he writes:

> Nature-creation does speak to us; but it tells us only what it is, and how it functions on its own. In other words, in nature the Creator shows us what he willed to exist and how it functions, but not how he wills the human person — *qua* human person — to use this existing reality. It is the human person, as a rational and prudent created being, who must interpret, evaluate and judge the realisation of the given nature from the moral point of view. ('Historicity and moral norm' in Raphael Gallagher and Brendan McConvery (eds), *History and Conscience* (Gill and Macmillan, 1989), p. 35)

This means that the word 'natural' in the term 'natural law' does not refer to natural in contradistinction to artificial. 'Natural' in 'natural law' really means 'reasonable'. In Chapter 3 we considered the eight dimensions of the nature of the human person, integrally and adequately considered. Living as befits a human person means living in a way which takes proper account of all these dimensions of human personhood. Living in this way is living reasonably. It is living in accordance with the natural law.

It is clear from the above that whatever the contraception debate in the Roman Catholic Church is about, it should not hinge on the fact that certain methods of contraception are 'artificial'. In itself that has no direct relevance to any natural law discussion. The mere fact that a procedure is 'artificial' does not mean that it is 'unnatural' in terms of the natural law. What is 'artificial' can in fact be more 'natural' in natural law terminology since it can be 'more reasonable'. The 1982 Report *Choices in Childlessness*, published by the Free Church Federal Council and the British Council of Churches, expressed this point very succinctly:

> ... the popular ethical distinction between the 'natural' and the 'unnatural' is a distinction between what is in keeping with human nature and what is not. It is not a distinction between the natural and the artificial. Since, then, human beings are by nature intelligent and creative, and the adaptation of the environment to their needs is an expression of their intelligence, human artifice, such as that developed in medical technology, is in principle ethically natural. (p. 42)

The significance and role of moral prohibitions

We saw earlier in the chapter that belief in certain fundamental human values implies the rejection of actions which are in direct violation of these values. In practice, as Kenny noted, and as Vatican II demonstrated in its statement on reverence for the human person, this means that any community committed to these basic values needs some sort of moral code. By articulating its prohibition or rejection of actions in flagrant violation of these values, the community commits itself to the upholding of these values. Whatever the debate about the theoretical absoluteness of such basic prohibitions, the community is saying that, in practice, there are no circumstances in which, in their eyes, such a prohibited action might justifiably be done. Hence as a community for all practical purposes they are prepared to uphold these prohibitions as absolute.

However, not all moral prohibitions in a community concern actions in flagrant violation of the dignity of the human person. Hence, not all moral prohibitions should be understood as absolute, not even those which use such expressions as 'intrinsically evil', or 'against the natural law'. A sound understanding of this point is of particular importance to Roman Catholics since they belong to a Church which has the practice of issuing teaching statements on moral issues which often contain prohibitions of this kind. To regard these prohibitions as absolute is probably to misinterpret the intention of those issuing the teaching and is certainly to misunderstand the role and significance of moral prohibitions for individual decision-making.

What role, then, do moral prohibitions of this kind play in our decision-making? Let us prescind from the possibility of disagreement with a particular prohibition. I discussed that in my article 'Conformity and dissent in the Church' (*The Way* (April 1988), pp. 87–101). It will also need to be considered in the epilogue. Let us assume, therefore, that we are dealing with a moral prohibition that we fully accept. Even in such a case the fact that the community subscribes to this prohibition does not render personal conscience redundant.

Of its very nature the moral prohibition in question will be 'universal'. Yet the situation to which it is to be applied is of its very nature 'particular'.Hence, a kind of dialectic between the universal and the particular comes into play here. This dialectic consists in the fact that no pre-packaged description in universal terms can fully describe a situation in all its particularity. Any such universal description will always leave a 'residue'. More can be said of this situation than is contained in this universal description. And sometimes this 'more' may be morally very significant — so much so, in certain cases, that the ethical evaluation of the action in this particular situation is drawn more from the residue than from the universal of which it is being considered as an instance.

When this happens, it would be inaccurate to interpret a person's conscience-decision, although not in accord with the prohibition, as either rejecting the prohibition or violating it. It does neither. It takes what the prohibition is saying fully into consideration. In other words, it takes full cognizance of the dimension of being human which this prohibition is designed to promote or safeguard. However, it perceives that another dimension of being human is also involved in this particular situation. Moreover, it judges that this other dimension of being human is either more important in itself or at least in this instance is touching a deeper level of what it means to be human. The prohibition serves its purpose by alerting the person to the fact that this action is unable to safeguard fully the first dimension of being human. The person's conscience gives proper respect to this first dimension by checking carefully to make sure that the human benefit to be achieved or human harm to be avoided is of sufficient importance to justify in this instance giving preference to this dimension of being human.

Some reflections on the Vatican prohibition of contraception

A moral prohibition that has obviously occasioned a major debate in the Roman Catholic Church is that which forbids artificial contraception. As is well known, the report of the Papal Commission which had originally been set up by John XXIII advised Paul VI that he would be more in conformity with the natural law basis of the Church's teaching on marriage and the family if he changed its position with regard to the prohibition of artificial contraception. In his 1968 encyclical letter *Humanae Vitae* Paul VI rejected their advice and reiterated that prohibition.

The prohibition of artificial contraception is an interesting example of the role of moral prohibitions in decision-making. That is why it is worth examining more closely. I have no intention of discussing the substance of Paul VI's teaching nor the strengths or weaknesses of the argumentation on which it is based. I looked at that side of the question in *Life and Love*, pp. 110–19. My purpose here is simply to use the prohibition of *Humanae Vitae* as an example of a universal prohibition of Catholic moral teaching.

It is very illuminating to examine how this prohibition is seen to relate to practical decision-making in the eyes of Gustave Martelet, a French Jesuit theologian, who is a strong supporter of the encyclical and who is completely convinced of the validity of its teaching. In fact, it is suggested by some commentators that Martelet actually had a hand in the composition of *Humanae Vitae*. Certainly, on the Sunday following the encyclical's publication Paul VI publicly singled out Martelet's book *Amour conjugal et renouveau conciliaire*, as offering a helpful explanation of the teaching of *Humanae Vitae* (cf. *Acta Apostolicae Sedis* (1990), p. 528, n. 1).

In an article published shortly after the encyclical came out, Martelet offered the following observation on the pastoral commentaries issued by most episcopal conferences throughout the world to guide their people in how to respond to the Pope's teaching at the level of their conscience-decisions. What he writes is of particular interest for our examination of the relationship between moral rules and the conscience-decision of the individual.

> All these episcopal interpretations simply insist that the encyclical could not suppress the responsibilities which the conscience of the couple must carry. *This is just as true in this case as it is in the case of every other law.* It is simply not true that the encyclical has really put this conscience in danger. But the manner in which it has generally been understood could certainly lead to this belief. In order to put an end in the Church to a point of view on contraception which is erroneous, Paul VI has had to speak in a language which unequivocally rejects an opinion which is truly harmful. In this the Pope has acted as moral guide for all men and women whom he alerts through the Church about a very real danger; in thus speaking to humankind, is he necessarily speaking directly to each individual as his personal moral guide? What seems to be true is that above all he wishes to denounce the errors of *principle* which are often committed in judgements made on situations of *fact* . . . He recalls the norm which is in danger of giving way: he does not specify the conditions to which this norm must be allowed to be accommodated. But neither does he deny them. He takes them for granted. ('Pour comprendre "Humanae Vitae"', *Nouvelle Revue Théologique* (1968), pp. 1014–16)

Obviously Martelet agrees with Paul VI rather than with the Papal Birth Control Commission regarding what the Church should say about artificial contraception. However, the significance he gives to the pope's prohibition of contraception *vis-à-vis* the role of conscience seems to be closely in line with what I have been suggesting above. He seems to be saying that, although artificial contraception is intrinsically wrong (*intrinsece inhonestum*: n. 14), yet a couple may decide in good faith that in their particular situation this is the right thing for them to do. Martelet, in his book *Existence et Amour*, writes with approval of the 1968 Pastoral Directives of the French Bishops. These directives offer a similar interpretation of how the moral prohibition of *Humanae Vitae* relates to the decision-making of couples:

> Contraception can never be a good thing. It is always something disordered, but this disorder is not always sinful. In fact, it can happen that husbands and wives believe themselves confronted with a real conflict of duties . . .
> On the one hand, they are conscious of the duty of respecting the openness to life of each conjugal act; likewise they consider their obligation in conscience to avoid or to put off until later a new birth, and they are deprived of the help of relying on biological rhythms. On the other hand, they do not see, as far as they are concerned, how they could at present renounce the physical expression of their love without endangering the stability of their marriage (*Gaudium et Spes*, n. 51.1).
> We will simply remind the faithful of the constant teaching of moral theology on this matter: when one has a choice of duties where, whatever decision is taken, one cannot avoid evil, traditional wisdom tries to ascertain before God which duty is the most important at this juncture . . .
> . . . the feeling of being torn between contradictory obligations is found, in one form or another, in the life of almost every home; that it is necessary to reconcile the physical and moral well-being of one partner with that of the other, the well-being of the children with that of the parents and even the well-being of each one of the children with that of his or her brothers and sisters, or the duty of one's calling with the demands of the home . . .
> This is on the whole the sad experience of the human condition. (n. 16) (Original French text in *Pour relire 'Humanae Vitae'* (Louvain: Duculot, 1970), pp. 154–5)

It is clear that the French bishops recognize that in artificial contraception a dimension of being human is being adversely affected.

However, they would recognize that this may not be the only or even the most important element of moral significance in artificial contraception. Although artificial contraception might be described as interfering in some way or other with our natural functioning as sexual persons, in many instances it can also be described as an indispensable and humanly beneficial means for enabling a deep and important exchange of faithful, interpersonal love to be shared between these two partners in their responsibly fruitful marriage. And the 'good' of this second description might be judged to be of much greater importance in terms of human well-being. A decision based on such a judgement would be regarded as both 'right' and 'good' in this particular instance.

Although Martelet is in full agreement with the teaching of *Humanae Vitae*, he does not interpret this teaching as involving an *absolute* prohibition of artificial contraception. This is clear from the fact that, like the French bishops, Martelet believes that a person can rightly decide in conscience that other more important values might justify the decision to use artificial contraception.

If Martelet and the French bishops are right about this, the post-*Humanae Vitae* debate about its implications for pastoral practice has been largely missing the point. That debate has been based on an assumption that *Humanae Vitae* articulates an *absolute* moral rule against artificial contraception. The Martelet interpretation would suggest that the *Humanae Vitae* rule against artificial contraception is *not an absolute rule*. In that case, what the debate should have focused on should have been: how precisely is the good of the human person adversely affected by artificial contraception? If that question could be answered more satisfactorily, it would be much easier to work out the moral equation which would also have to take account of the human benefit achieved through the use of artificial contraception and both the positive and negative aspects of natural methods of birth control.

In the first section of this chapter we looked at the role of experience in the on-going task of formulating moral norms. That has implications for the kind of decision we have been considering in this section. If experience shows that such a 'good and right' decision to use contraception is repeated time and time again or is even part of a general mind-set in the lives of very many Christian married couples, this could be an indication that the moral ruling would be better formulated in terms of the positive evaluation brought out by the second description than in terms of the negative evaluation found in the first description. This would be a case of a ruling being reformulated in the light of experience and new knowledge and insight. It could be an instance of what Cardinal Hume was referring to at the Synod in Rome when he said that the experience of married people can be 'an authentic source of theology from which we, the pastors, and indeed the whole Church can draw'. In fact, this was precisely the suggestion made by the Papal Birth Control Commission, a suggestion which Paul VI felt unable to accept. In the Pastoral Introduction to its report to the pope, the Commission actually suggested a formula for presenting its revised ruling to the Church in general. The whole makes interesting reading. In the light of what we are considering the following passage is particularly significant:

> Today, thanks to the progress made in reflection on the subject, and without in any way detracting from the importance of procreation, which, allied to true love, is one of the ends of marriage, we have a clearer view of the multiple responsibilities of married couples: towards each other, first, so that they can live a love that leads them to unity; towards their children, whose development and education . . . they must assure; then towards the institution of marriage, whose stability (cf. 1 Cor 7:10–11) and unity they are to maintain through the quality of their love and respect for each other's dignity (cf. 1 Pet 3:1–7); and finally towards society, since the family is its basic unit.
>
> All this creates a complex of obligations which, far from eliminating duties, invites one to take account of them so that they can all be undertaken together as far as is humanly possible, with due respect for their hierarchy and relative importance . . .
>
> What has been condemned in the past and remains so today is . . . the rejection of procreation as a specific task of marriage. In the past, the Church could not speak other than she did, because the problem of birth control did not confront human consciousness is the same way. Today, having clearly recognized the legitimacy and even the duty of regulating births, she recognizes too that human intervention in the process of the marriage act for reasons drawn from the finality of marriage itself should not always be excluded, provided that the criteria of morality are always safeguarded.
>
> If an arbitarily contraceptive mentality is to be condemned, as has always been the Church's view, an intervention to regulate conception in a spirit of true, reasonable and generous charity . . . does not deserve to be, because if it were, other goods of marriage might be endangered.
>
> As for the means that husband and wife can legitimately employ, it is their task to decide these together, without drifting into arbitrary decisions, but always taking account of the objective criteria of morality. These criteria are in the first place those that relate to the totality of

married life and sexuality. (Peter Harris and others, *On Human Life: An Examination of 'Humanae Vitae'* (Burns & Oates, 1968), pp. 218–20)

In this section I may seem to have been going over old ground. However, I believe that the general point I have been illustrating through this example is of importance far beyond any particular consideration of the Church's prohibition of artificial contraception.

One final example

Another very instructive example of a moral prohibition is that which forbids mutilation, whether of oneself or of someone else. Mutilation involves violating a person's bodily integrity and bodily integrity pertains to our well-being as a bodily person. To lose our bodily integrity by, for instance, having a leg amputated or an eye removed is to suffer an evil. However, some instances of mutilation can also be described as therapeutic amputation for the sake of the health of the whole person. This brings out the fact that particular human actions can be labelled with a number of different universal descriptions, some more ethically significant than others.

In the case of amputation our forebears learned from experience that mutilation, though a violation of bodily integrity and so normally to be avoided, can in some instances be the only way of saving a person's life. So they were able to supplement the moral prohibition 'mutilation is wrong' by adding on an additional rider 'except when such a mutilation is needed to save that person's life or overall health'. That seemed to provide a sufficient guide to cover cases of mutilation.

However, some years ago organ transplantation from a living donor became a possibility. Wise and loving people were in no doubt that it was not only morally good but even heroically unselfish for a person to offer to sacrifice an organ, a kidney for instance, the loss of which would not endanger life or seriously impair bodily activity. However, the moral prohibition of mutilation, even with the supplementary rider added, excluded such a possibility. Hence, experience taught us that the prohibition needed to be reformulated still further to allow for this kind of organ transplantation. This reformulation allowed mutilation for the additional reason of helping another person, provided what was being sacrificed was only 'non-substantial integrity'. This would be the case when there is only partial curtailment of organic function through the donation of one of our double organs (e.g. an eye, an ovary or a kidney).

However, even that was not the end of the story. With the great advances made in recent years in the transplantation of organs from dead donors there is no longer the same justification for the mutilation involved in organic transplantation from a living donor. So once again the prohibition had to be modified and yet another rider was put in stating that the mutilation involved in organ donation was not justified if the same result could be obtained through the transplantation of a cadaver organ.

It is clear, therefore, that in the case of some moral prohibitions there is a constant process of modification going on which enables the prohibition to be adapted to meet the needs of new or changing situations. As pointed out by Albert R. Jonsen and Stephen Toulmin, *The Abuse of Casuistry: A History of Moral Reasoning* (University of California, 1988), this is why casuistry, in some form or other, is so important in moral theology. Despite its misuse by some casuists in the past and the consequent abuse showered on it by Pascal, casuistry plays an important role in the process of refining our practical moral principles. When it fell into disgrace after Pascal's onslaught, the stage was left free for an unbridled absolutism to take over. This marked a very unhealthy period in the history of moral theology. The current retrieval of a healthy casuistry has been at least partially due to the increasing complexity of the problems to be faced in the field of medical ethics. Perhaps this is another instance of 'foreign prophecy'!

The need for moral prohibitions to be modified in the light of new experience is an obvious consequence of our appreciation of the historical and cultural dimension of being a human person. To recognize this is to free ourselves to be open to new and perhaps richer and more relevant articulations of what it means to be human today. Such articulations may in turn lead us to modify our moral prohibitions. To deny this is to risk closing our ears to any fresh challenge from God inviting us to be human in ways more appropriate to the needs and opportunities of today's world.

Good decisions

Christian conscience-formation is concerned with both our personal openness to God's call and the concrete decisions we take by way of responding to God's call in particular situations. In one sense, our personal openness is the more important dimension. Yet that must not be reduced to the level of mere good intention, the proverbial paving of hell itself! Personal openness implies a real commitment to discover God's will. This commitment implies a willingness to do all I can to make sure that my decision is such that it will really bring about human well-being in this situation seen in its broader context. Put simply, it means that I have to take all the steps appropriate to the importance of this decision to make sure that it is wise and loving. A responsible Christian decision has to avoid the two extremes of a mindless obedience to external authority and a purely individualistic and blinkered reliance on my own opinion, regardless of the accumulated experience, wisdom and love of my fellow Christians and the rest of the human family. Provided my decision has been made responsibly, it can be said to be 'morally good', even though later experience might eventually show me that it was misguided or even wrong.

Of course, this emphasis on the 'goodness' of my decision does not imply that 'right' decisions do not matter. They certainly do, since what is at stake in 'rightness/wrongness' is whether my decision *actually* promotes human well-being or not, and that is a matter of concern both to us humans and to God himself. Nevertheless, our personal openness to God's call does not imply that our decision will always be 'right'. That would be an impossibility for fallible human beings and, in any case, even 'rightness' itself can have a historical component, both at a cultural and a personal level. However, our personal openness to God's call implies that we do all we can to make sure that our decision is the 'best' we can make in the circumstances.

I believe that the approach to morality I have just outlined is very much in line with the direction in which Vatican II has pointed us. This approach denies that all that counts from a moral point of view is a person's good intention. Some actions motivated by compassion, for instance, can in reality be very destructive of persons. This view holds, therefore, that whether certain states of affairs or ways of acting are conducive to human betterment is a question of *fact*. To that extent it is ready to acknowledge that we need to learn from experience and that there is great truth in the well-worn dictum, 'time alone will tell'.

'God's will' is to be found in our creative reading of the situations that face us in life. Obviously, this creative reading of life is not some élitist activity reserved to people with a high IQ or a privileged education. An important ingredient of it is 'good will'. This does not mean a vacuous good intention which bears no relation to the way a person is actually living his or her life. On the contrary, it means a genuine commitment to the basic human goods which spell out the general direction in which human well-being is to be found. A person of 'good will' may not be able to articulate very accurately what these goods are. Nor may such a person necessarily have either the wisdom or experience to discern how best these goods are to be pursued in every situation facing him or her. What is demanded, however, is a lived-out commitment, despite failures and inconsistencies, to pursue these basic human goods to the best of one's ability.

Such a commitment is integral to what true conscience is all about. Moreover, because the human person is essentially interdependent, our conscientious search for the truth in moral living will be, in the words of Cardinal Ratzinger, 'a community effort, in which human beings joined in space and time help each other to discover better what is difficult to discover on one's own' (Address to College of Cardinals, *Origins* (25 April 1991), p. 755). Conscience, therefore, will be true to its original meaning *'cum-scire'* (shared knowing). Moral principles and prohibitions, as we have seen, also have their proper place in this shared knowing. They are, as it were, abbreviations of tradition.

This commitment to the truly human well-being of others and oneself is essential if a person is to lay claim to 'conscience' in any proper sense of the world. Without such a commitment any claim to be 'following one's conscience' is a misuse of language. It is substituting the idol of self-will in place of true conscience. When a human decision is the product of true conscience, however, it is aptly termed 'morally good', even though it might eventually be seen to be misguided or mistaken and so might also be described as 'morally wrong' (i.e. incorrect). This links in with the point made in Chapter 2. Goodness and badness are properly attributed only to persons. They apply to our being human at its most *personal* level. Personal goodness or badness refers to the kind of person we choose to be through the on-going process of responding to the demands of life in the way we behave towards other persons and ourselves.

Chapter 5

MORAL THEOLOGY — NOT TRULY HUMAN WITHOUT THE FULL PARTICIPATION OF WOMEN

Women's experience — historical and cultural

Persons do not exist in the abstract. We are beings whose existence is necessarily bound up with history and culture. This is true both of ourselves and also of our knowledge of ourselves. Our very experience is historically and culturally conditioned as is our ability to reflect on that experience.

Although the perception of this truth cannot be attributed specifically to the insights of women, nevertheless it is a truth on which they have laid great insistence. It provides the base on which they lay the main foundation of feminist theology, namely that Christian theology is substantially flawed because it has been constructed predominantly by men and in the light of men's experience of a world in which women were second-rate citizens and women's experience was not considered theologically important.

This has brought about multiple levels of distortion. Not only has women's experience not been listened to. The very experience itself has been distorted. The rich possibilities of human experience which should have been open to women as much as to men have been largely denied to them by the male shapers of society, culture and Church who have imposed their less-than-fully-human perception of women on the thinking and structures throughout most of history. Consequently, women's experience has been diminished and impoverished. It has been distorted by a continuing element of oppression which has militated against their being empowered to make their full contribution to human life and understanding. At the same time, obviously, there has been a corresponding distortion which has affected men's experience too. If we are essentially interdependent beings, to misinterpret this interdependence in the way patriarchy has ends up with both men and women experiencing their humanity in a distorted way. Moreover, the listening to and inter-

pretation of this distorted human experience has been principally
done by men and that in its turn has contributed a further level of
distortion.

In the light of this, women theologians are insisting that women's
experience, diverse though it is bound to be, must be firmly in place
on the theological agenda. Moreover, women must be fully — not
just tokenly — represented wherever theological analysis and interpretation is being undertaken. An indication of what this might
mean in practice can be seen in the choice of themes for some of the
issues of the international theological periodical *Concilium* published since 1985. Four whole issues have been devoted to the
following topics: *Women — Invisible in Church and Theology*
(n. 182), *Women, Work and Poverty* (n. 194), *Motherhood:
Experience, Institution, Theology* (n. 206) and *The Special Nature
of Women* (1991/6). Moreover, apart from a bulletin note by
Gregory Baum in *Motherhood*, the contributors in each case have
all been women theologians.

The perception of motherhood as a topic for theological analysis
is itself very significant but the way it is tackled is even more
illuminating. What in a male-orientated theology has tended to be
presented uncritically as pertaining to what would be seen as the
'nature' of womanhood is analysed much more critically by women
theologians who are careful to listen to women's experience of
motherhood as an institution. This revised agenda for a theological
consideration of motherhood is spelled out clearly by Anne Carr
and Elisabeth Schüssler Fiorenza in the opening paragraphs of their
joint Editorial:

> In this number of *Concilium* we explore motherhood as a theological
> concept in the light of Adrienne Rich's important distinction between the
> potential relationship of every woman to her powers of reproduction
> and to children on the one hand, and motherhood as a social, cultural,
> and religious institution and ideology on the other. It is the institution of
> motherhood that keeps this potential, and women and children, under
> patriarchal control, and disempowers women. This distinction between
> experience and institution provides the basis for feminist analysis of
> motherhood as a source for theological reflection.
>
> Our intention in dealing with the theme of motherhood as experience,
> institution and theology is to expose some of the ways in which patri-
> archal sexism has shaped cultural, religious and Christian under-
> standings of women and to indicate some of the critical perspectives
> which feminist theory affords today. It is our hope that in the light of
> these perspectives on the differences, indeed contradictions, between

experience and institution that a critical feminist theological reflection
on motherhood might be developed. (p. 3)

There is no doubt that many male theologians in the Church are
trying to listen to the voice of women and take on board the insights
they are sharing with us. This is also true of those who issue authoritative statements in the name of the Church. Nevertheless, more
than listening is needed. A radical conversion of our way of per-
ceiving reality is needed. For instance, the pope's recent Apostolic
Letter on *The Dignity of Woman* (1988) affirms very strongly the
rights of women as human persons and insists on their 'essential
equality' with men. Clearly, John Paul II has been trying to listen to
the signs of the times. However, women have noted that his listening
does not yet seem to have achieved the more radical conversion that
is needed. In her *Notes on Moral Theology*, Lisa Sowle Cahill comments: 'While the pope opposes discrimination against women, he
fails to ask critically whether stereotypical definitions of "feminine"
nature — here cast after a romantic ideology of mother-love — are
part of the problem' (*Theological Studies* (March 1990), p. 58). The
experience of women has led them to be highly suspicious of an
approach which would view them as 'equal but different'. In practice, this 'difference' tends to be cashed in the currency of inequality
when the difference is identified as motherhood and this in turn is
interpreted as motherhood *as institution*. Vatican II has insisted that
the dignity of the human person lies at the very heart of Christian
morality: 'There is a growing awareness of the exalted dignity
proper to the human person, since she stands above all things, and
her rights and duties are universal and inviolable' (*Gaudium et Spes*,
n. 26). Acceptance of this foundational principle at this point in
history obliges us to recognize that one of the major signs of our
times is the crying need fully to accept and work out at all levels of
life the full and equal humanity of both men and women. That being
the case, we can appreciate why Margaret Farley offers the following principle as a test of the authenticity of our commitment to the
dignity of every human person:

> Whatever diminishes or denies the full humanity of women must be
> presumed not to reflect the divine or an authentic relation to the divine,
> or to reflect the authentic nature of things, or to be the message or work
> of an authentic redeemer or a community of redemption.

It is in the light of such a moral principle that another woman
theologian, Christine Gudorf, spells out what she would con-

sider to be the minimum criteria for a responsible ethic of motherhood:

> Minimum criteria for an ethic of motherhood must include: (1) respect for women's rights to make decisions in their lives: on marriage, sex, work, and contraception; (2) the opening of female roles to alternatives including but not requiring motherhood and child care; (3) respect for women, their bodies, their control of their bodies and for sexual interaction as mutuality not domination; (4) acceptance by men of equal responsibility for child care, housework, and financial support of children; (5) social support for parenting: paid maternity leave and affordable quality daycare; (6) open, non-coercive access for all women to a variety of safe, effective means of contraception; (7) social support for lowering and equalizing maternal and infant mortality rates by addressing poverty which afflicts women and children most. ('Women's choice for motherhood: beginning a cross-cultural approach', *Concilium*, n. 206, p. 61)

Embodiment

It is often asserted that it is part of the 'nature' of women to be more in touch with their bodies. It is alleged that this is because only women have a menstrual cycle and can become pregnant and both these experiences can have a major impact on a woman's personal and social life-style. Some extreme feminists have even argued that one of their aims should be to free women from being the slaves of their bodies. Most women writers, however, reject such a view. They see it as colluding still further in an attitude which would regard the male as the model and the female as an inferior product, burdened with this second-rate body for functional purposes to keep the human race going. This negative attitude would be reflected, for instance, in the way menstruation is sometimes referred to as 'the curse' and a woman's menstrual flow has in many cultures and religious traditions been regarded as 'unclean' and an occasion of religious defilement.

Women today are more ready to accept the giftedness of their bodies. They are happy to celebrate the positive goodness of their bodies precisely as *their own* and not merely as found desirable by men. They would even argue that men have tended to be too 'disembodied' in their thinking and in this way have presented only a partial reading of reality. Women would stress the importance of feelings as an essential dimension of our being human and a dimension with profound moral implications. In a thought-provoking essay with the tantalizing title 'The power of anger in the work of love', Beverly Harrison writes:

> . . . the assumption [that] many moral theologians make [is] that we are most moral when most detached and disengaged from life-struggle. Far too many Christian ethicists continue to imply that 'disinterestedness' and 'detachment' are basic preconditions for responsible moral action. And in the dominant ethical tradition, moral rationality too often is *disembodied* rationality. (In Carol S. Robb (ed.), *Making the Connections: Essays in Feminist Social Ethics* (Boston: Beacon Press, 1985), p. 13)

Harrison goes on to argue that 'all our knowledge, including our moral knowledge, is body-mediated knowledge'. We know and value the world through our ability to touch, to hear, to see it. Our ideas are 'dependent on our sensuality'. Hence, she lays great stress on the importance of feeling. 'When we cannot feel, literally, we lose our connection to the world . . . If feeling is damaged or cut off, our power to image the world and act into it is destroyed and our rationality is impaired . . .' A realization of the importance of this dimension is one of the gifts that women theologians are bringing to the field of moral theology.

> A feminist moral theology enables us to recognize that a major source of rising moral insensitivity derives from being out-of-touch with our bodies. Many people live so much in their heads that they no longer feel their connectedness to other living things. (p. 13)

Harrison goes on to use anger as an example of the point she is making:

> It is my thesis that we Christians have come very close to killing love precisely because we have understood anger to be a deadly sin. Anger is not the opposite of love. It is better understood as a feeling signal that all is not well in our relation to other persons or groups or to the world around us. Anger is a mode of connectedness to others and it is always a vivid form of caring . . .
> Where anger rises, there the energy to act is present. In anger, one's body-self is engaged, and the signal comes that something is amiss in relation . . . We must never lose touch with the fact that all serious human activity, especially action for social change, takes its bearing from the rising power of human anger. Such anger is a signal that change is called for, that transformation in relation is required. (pp. 14–15)

In the section of Chapter 3 which looked at the 'embodied' dimension of being a human person I quoted David Lonsdale's editorial in

The Way (1990) where he makes a similar point. In the same issue of *The Way* Rosemary Haughton has a haunting piece entitled 'Godly anger and beyond' (pp. 114–23). She argues that few people can maintain indefinitely this godly anger in the face of continued injustice. The danger is that eventually 'burn-out' will occur, bringing with it cynicism and despair. She believes that such 'burn-out' is not inevitable, however, provided attention is paid to what she calls 'the work of endurance'. By this she means keeping the hope which fires the anger alive under the ashes.

Christian moral theology must not be reduced to an exploration of moral concepts, however interesting that might be. An essential feature of it must be an involvement in reading the signs of the times for our world today so that these signs can be appropriately responded to. As David Tracy puts it, it is not just a matter of knowing (what he calls a 'manifestation disclosure'); it is also a call to 'transformation'. That is why moral theology must be experience-based. The signs of the times are not restricted to the world of ideas. They include the joys and hopes, the sufferings and fears of human persons and the human family. The signs of the times have to be *felt*. They are the way the human spirit, moved by God's own Spirit, recoils in horror from whatever is dehumanizing and violating respect for persons in our world today. The signs of the times are *movements* of the human spirit. They embody human emotions of anger, repugnance, horror, fear, anxiety as well as the positive emotions of hope, expectation, determination, courage, etc. A disembodied moral theology will be oblivious to the real signs of the times.

Naturally, women theologians are not advocating an abandonment of human reason. Beverly Harrison, for instance, in the essay quoted above, stresses that feelings in themselves do not tell us what we should do. As she puts it: 'The moral question is not "what do I feel?" but rather "what do I do with what I feel?"'. Of themselves feelings do not lead automatically to wise and loving action. Harrison stresses that 'it is part of the deeper work of ethics to help us move through all our feelings to adequate strategies of moral action'.

In an article entitled 'Feminism and spatiality: ethics and the recovery of a hidden dimension' in the *Journal of Feminist Studies in Religion* (1988, pp. 55–71) H. Shannon Jung conducts a similar exercise to this chapter and listens to the experience of women with regard to what he calls the 'spatial' nature of our being embodied human persons. He claims that many women writers have identified the strengths arising from women's spatiality and, in so doing, have empowered all persons to appreciate the spatial dimension of their human existence. Jung locates this 'spatiality' in four dimensions: affectivity, particularity, limitation and relation to others. These dimensions, he claims, have all been downgraded in favour of their opposites.

His examination of particularity and limitation throws further light on the notion of embodiment. He notes that a number of women writers have commented on women's tendency to be involved with 'concrete feelings, things and people rather than abstract entities'. Attention is focused on *particular* others. 'An ethic of care seems more attuned to the particularity of the situation rather than to the rights of interchangeable others' (p. 62). In terms of an ethic based on interdependence this ties in with Carol Gilligan's observation that women veer more towards an ethic of *care* rather than one based on abstract rights.

Jung notes that Rosemary Ruether observes that this gift makes women less prone to become prisoners of ideological thinking (p. 63). Emphasis on the particular highlights the richness of variety. Again Jung notes: 'Without an appreciation of particularity, we may ignore unique aspects of people and things, or simply project our own preferences or values onto them' (p. 62).

Flowing from this emphasis on embodied affectivity and its consequent attention to the particular, there flows an appreciation of the limitedness of human life. This has important implications for moral theology, as Jung brings out forcefully:

> We cannot be everywhere or do everything . . . We cannot do more than is in our power, power that is bounded by our hereness. Spatiality locates us in a here that cannot simultaneously be there. Though such limits may be frustrating if perceived only negatively, there is a positive side to this reality. Spatiality constitutes enablement; we live within the contours of our situation. Ignoring that basic fact of our spatiality can be a major source of delusion, frustration, or grandiosity.
>
> Women have been more comfortable with the fact of limitation than men. The positive result of this has been that women have been more in touch with the concrete reality of bodily and social limitations. Rather than the 'drives toward possession, conquest, and accumulation' that Ruether associates with patriarchal society, feminists should emphasize 'the values of reciprocity and acceptance of mutual limitation'. (pp. 62–3)

An example of a woman's positive acceptance of the limitedness of human existence and the transforming impact of this positive attitude is found in an extraordinarily powerful book written out of the crucifying experience of personal and family suffering. The writer, Margaret Spufford, says that 'The acceptance of limitation seems to me one of the most important, and also one of the most dangerous, of disciplines' (p. 90). She then proceeds to describe most movingly what that has come to mean to her in her own particular life experience:

> It may be tempting, in chronic pain, to give up on the body, to despair of it; but the Word was made flesh. It seemed, and seems, important to me that the incarnate Christ came to us, and into our world of ramshackle bodies. Mine is so very ramshackle that sometimes it is difficult to be patient with it, but I do try. I enjoy material things a lot, which helps. It is only the *wrongness* I object to. I loathe and detest my bone disease. I am often miserable, often shamefully discontented, often isolated, often lonely. I fear pain, and the fear does not grow less. But oddly, after twenty years, I can no longer wish that things were quite otherwise, except for my husband's sake. Learning to live with the disorder as creatively as possible has in the end formed the person I am. I cannot, in the last resort, regret being the person I am, as historian, or mother, or oblate. I think I can say, without any trace of masochism, that the disease has indeed been a creative medium. (*Celebration*, p. 93)

Some years ago at a meeting of moral theologians I delivered a paper entitled 'On starting from where people are'. My theme was that very often moral theology seems to be saying to people 'You should not be where you are. You ought to be somewhere else!' This struck me as most unhelpful, especially in situations like that of people who were divorced and remarried. I am intrigued by the way women's insistence on recognizing our limitation throws light on this sense of uneasiness about the way moral theology approached such problems. If moral theology took this insight seriously, I feel sure it would throw new light on quite a variety of so-called 'conflict situations' in life.

In summary, therefore, although female embodiment might be experienced differently in different cultures, the overall emphasis put on embodiment by women theologians questions some of the assumptions of a moral theology which has been developed almost exclusively by males. It challenges any tendency to think of moral reasoning as an exercise in disembodied rationality. It reminds us, too, of the importance of listening to our feelings and emotions, if we are to understand what is going on. It also helps us to appreciate the 'spatial' dimension of our human existence, especially our particularity and the essential limitedness of a person's life and its opportunities.

Moral agency

Women often point out that gender stereotyping portrays women as *passive* and men as *active*. The utter untruth of this caricature is obvious when we think how it is nearly always women who have had to 'cope' in the struggle for survival. When what an oppressive patriarchal culture designates as 'women's work' (child-care, house-work etc.) is taken into account, women are far more 'active' than men and in general carry out most 'work' done by human beings. Yet women are still stereotyped as 'passive' and this is carried over into the moral field. The moral agency of women is downgraded. They are regarded as unreliable moral agents because they are reputed not to think clearly, being dominated by their emotions and too easily influenced by particular situations.

One of the challenges coming from women theologians today is that moral theology needs to rethink its whole approach to moral agency. Some fascinating work, relevant to this point, has been done by the social scientist Carol Gilligan. She challenges the criteria for judging a person's growth in maturity as a moral agent as presented by Lawrence Kohlberg in his writing on the stages of moral development. Gilligan questions the basic assumption of Kohlberg that the goal of moral development lies in an individual's achieving complete autonomy. That would imply that we are more truly human to the extent that we become increasingly more independent. Apparently, women have come out badly in comparison to men in tests conducted according to Kohlberg's criteria. Gilligan has tried to demonstrate that Kohlberg's criteria are suspect on the grounds that they are drawn from an individualist and power-orientated attitude which is characteristic of many men today — and perhaps down through the ages too. Moreover, his research is based exclusively on male experience. Women's experience would point to a somewhat different criterion for assessing moral development.

Reflecting on their experience, women have helped to bring to human consciousness the core insight that the heart of moral agency lies not in individual independence but in mutual interdependence. This is not just a preference for interdependence rather than independence. It is something based not on choice but on who we are as persons. It comes from a richer understanding of our being. It is flying in the face of reality to think that we are independent beings. We are essentially interdependent and in the age in which we are living we are getting a much better understanding of how deep this interdependence goes. Our decisions and the kind of person we are does not just affect other persons. Their effect on the environment and on other creatures reveals our fundamental interdependence with the rest of creation too. It is noteworthy how this interdependence insight from women's experience ties in with a similar insight which is part of the ecological 'signs of the times'. Of course, to highlight interdependence does not imply that personal freedom is not of immense importance. However, it insists that personal freedom has meaning and reality only in and through the medium of interdependence.

Beverly Harrison brings out the theological significance of this core insight about interdependence. She is one of many women theologians who draw attention to a way of thinking which sees God as unchanging, all-sufficient, unfeeling and invulnerable. It is an image of God, the great Loner. This is a God made in the image of the male philosophers and theologians. It is not the God of the Judeo-Christian revelation and certainly not the God of the women theologians. They want to reclaim the Christian God who is revealed as a God whose very being involves a unity-in-mutuality which is mind-blowing in terms of our human experience of unity and interdependence. Women theologians want to remind the rest of us that the God in whose image we are made thrives upon a richness of relational diversity which is but dimly reflected in the ambiguity of our own human longing to achieve oneness in and through our relationships.

Interdependence means more than that our decisions and the kind of persons we are affect other people and other creatures. It also works in the opposite direction. The kind of person I am is largely determined by the influence on me of other persons and the wider world. This has implications for my freedom too. Freedom is not merely an absence of external coercion. My freedom depends on a combination of my internal capacity for self-expression and personal choice and my external opportunities for actually exercising that capacity. Both these depend to a large extent on other people. I am not free to be a mechanic if I lack the necessary skills and if there is no opportunity for me to acquire those skills as well as no possibility of my exercising them, given my having acquired them. I am not free to be an open, loving person if my upbringing has left me closed, fearful and insecure. I cannot achieve freedom in these and other areas without the liberating action of other people.

This emphasis on interdependence forces us to face up to the social dimension of moral agency. This is not just saying that social factors have an influence on my development and decision-making as a moral agent. It is also saying that I am never a moral agent just on my own as an isolated individual. My very power to make decisions is itself an empowerment by others.

To view moral agency in this light brings out what Beverly Harrison refers to as the 'formidable power' of nurturing:

> We do not yet have a moral theology that teaches us the awe-ful, awe-some truth that we have the power through acts of love or lovelessness literally to create one another . . . Because we do not understand love as the power to act-each-other-into-well-being, we also do not under-stand the depth of our power to thwart life and to maim each other. That fateful choice is ours, either to set free the power of God's love in the world or to deprive each other of the very basis of personhood and community . . .
>
> It is within the power of human love to build up dignity and self-respect in each other or to tear each other down . . . Through acts of love directed to us, we become self-respecting and other-regarding persons, and we cannot be one without the other. If we lack self-respect, we also become the sorts of people who can neither see nor hear each other. (In Carol S. Robb (ed.), *Making the Connections*, pp. 11–12)

Developing the thought of the final sentence quoted above, Harrison goes on to stress that what is at stake here is not just the development of personhood but also the formation of community:

> For better or worse, women have had to face the reality that we have the power not only to create personal bonds between people but, more basically, to build up and deepen personhood itself. And to build up 'the person' is also to deepen relationship, that is, to bring forth community. (p. 11)

Another term used by women writers to express this important insight is *mutuality*. We are bound together by a web of mutually interlocking relationships. That is part of the very being of each of us. It belongs to the reality of each of us. Carol Gilligan's research came up with two interesting results on this point. They concerned the image of the web and the impact created by the word 'dependent'. She found that men tended to feel threatened by the image of a web. They saw it as a trap, taking away their freedom and independence. Women, on the other hand, tended to see the web as a very positive image, highlighting the way we are not left in isolation but bound to each other in relationships of mutual interdependence.

The reader will note that I have spoken of 'tendencies' of men and women. The women writers who draw our attention to this fact of experience would not want to claim that it proves the existence of innate gender stereotypes and that women and men are imprisoned by exclusive and unalterable gender characteristics. For instance, I doubt whether any woman could improve on what Nicholas Peter Harvey has written about our essential interdependence as human persons. He even applies the 'web' image to the whole of reality:

> I am either one with all creation, linked indivisibly with everyone and everything else, or I am nothing but illusion. It is not that I exist only in relationship, it is that I *am* relationship from the beginning. At no point can I stand outside the web, for there is nowhere to stand. (*The Morals of Jesus* (Darton, Longman & Todd, 1991), p. 61)

As regards the word 'dependent', men tend to look on that as denoting an undesirable feature in a person's make-up, a failure to be fully independent and autonomous. Consequently, the word 'dependent' is used in a pejorative sense as in the phrase, 'the dependency culture'. Women, on the other hand, tend to react much more favourably to the word 'dependent'. For them it speaks more of a person being 'dependable', someone you can rely on. This is an extremely important quality when our very being is understood as being located essentially in a network of interdependent relationships. At this level being dependent and being dependable reflects a dimension of being human which is indispensable for healthy personal and communal living.

What is objectionable about the dependency culture, therefore, is not the fact that people are naturally dependent on each other but the destruction of natural networks of interdependence by an intrusive and impersonal central bureaucracy. That fails to respect the kind of persons we are as human beings. A culture which destroys natural networks of interdependence and reduces people to a freedom-denying dependence on a central bureaucracy should be rejected as inhuman.

The emphasis women theologians place on interdependence has

implications for the issue of abortion too. For instance, Mary B. Mahowald writes:

> To treat the pregnant woman as an isolated individual, standing alone in her decision, is insulting in that it strips her of the very context that is integral to her identity. It may be less insulting to define her identity in the limited context of her family. The reality to address, however, is that the pregnant woman stands at the centre of multiple social relationships, some of which may be deeper than familial. The fulfillment of her individuality is intimately linked with all such relationships, as well as with her fetus. Her morality is similarly linked with those relationships . . .
>
> Because life is not lived by individuals in isolation from one another, but as an ongoing, complex system of interpersonal relationships, a really pro-life position does not affirm the life of the fetus alone or the pregnant woman alone; it affirms the life of the community in which they both participate. (In Sidney and Daniel Callahan (eds), *Abortion: Understanding Differences* (Plenum, 1984), pp. 113, 180)

Obviously, what conclusions are drawn from that statement will depend on how the human status of the fetus is interpreted. Writing in the same volume, Lisa Sowle Cahill links interdependence with embodiment: 'The body makes peculiar demands, creates peculiar relationships, and grounds peculiar obligations' (p. 268). Because of this link she notes that we can sometimes be bound by obligations to which we have not explicitly consented. Cahill suggests that the mother–fetus relationship comes into this category, even though she does not conclude from this that abortion can never be a defensible moral choice for a woman.

Still within this insight of interdependence as an essential aspect of moral agency, women approach the human reality of 'power' from a different angle. Power has tended to be seen as power over someone, and this has had practical consequences for the way a whole variety of relationships were understood. Those under authority were called 'subjects' and obedience tended to be seen as the subjection of one person's will to that of his or her 'superior'. Even the marriage relationship was viewed in this way. In fact, in many cultures and over many centuries a married woman was regarded as the property of her husband and Christian wives were obliged to promise obedience to their husbands.

The notion of interdependence changes the whole focus of the power relationship. A truly human exercise of power lies more in the direction of *empowerment*. Beverly Harrison, in the passage quoted above, is writing about the power of love. We have the awesome power to love each other into fuller personhood. This opens up a much richer understanding of the sexual relationship as 'life-giving'. It is life-giving in the first instance to the couple themselves. Moreover, their mutual life-giving love for each other not only can empower new life into existence but can also offer the most promising (though not the only) personal environment for empowering this new life to develop into fuller personhood, growing in wisdom and love before people and God.

This even has implications for the handling of disagreement which we are exploring in this book. The power syndrome would approach disagreement in terms of an argument to be won. The person with whom one disagrees is seen as one's opponent. Some moral theology manuals, following an earlier tradition, used to call those who disagreed with their position *adversarii*. The mutuality and empowerment approach sees a disagreement as an opportunity for mutual enrichment. The 'other' is someone to be listened to as she may be in touch with an aspect of truth to which I am not paying sufficient attention. That is why listening is a positive and active process. I am not out to try to trap the other person. I want to understand what this person is trying to say and so I am anxious to help her say it as clearly as possible. The point of the exchange is not to defeat the other but to try to move from disagreement towards agreement. The current emphasis on dialogue is very much in line with the approach of women theologians.

In summary, therefore, our understanding of the human person as moral agent is greatly enriched in the light of the experience and reflection of women. They warn us that to see ourselves as individuals, each concentrated on the attainment of his or her own autonomy, is an impoverished understanding of the human person. The essential interdependence of human persons gives a much richer view of moral agency. We empower each other rather than seek to dominate over each other. We approach each other as persons bonded together in mutual dependence rather than as competitors to be vanquished in the struggle for existence.

Conclusion

While I was preparing to write this chapter, I was meditating on the passage in John's gospel where the writer puts on to the lips of Jesus the night before he died the very powerful promise: 'When the Spirit of truth comes he will lead you to the complete truth, since he will not be speaking as from himself but will only say what he has learnt; and he will tell you of the things to come' (John 16:31). This spoke to me in terms of Vatican II's insistence that we must 'read the signs of the times' if we are to present a Gospel which is Good News for our contemporary world. This reading the signs of the times is a double process. It involves listening to the cry of the oppressed in our world today and it also involves discerning the movement of the Spirit in the midst of the oppressed as they struggle towards liberation.

What women are saying and writing on ethical issues touches both these levels. They are giving voice to an increasing awareness of oppression which is the experience of most women and has been such for most of recorded history. They are also creating a vision of a world without this oppression and through a combination of experimenting with new life-styles and rethinking traditional moral assumptions they are accepting the challenge of making this vision a reality in our world today.

If all of us, men and women together, are to understand the Gospel insofar as it is Good News for our world today, we must be open to what is happening among women. What is demanded is much more than that the institutional Church should cease to play its part in the oppression of women. What is needed is a recognition that unless we listen to the prophetic voices of women, we shall fail to appreciate the meaning of being human as it is being revealed to us today. Oppression is dehumanizing — and not just for those who are oppressed. It is also dehumanizing, perhaps even more so, for the oppressors since it is a form of blindness, an inability to recognize and live the truth. The truth that women are revealing to us today is not just about the liberation of women. It is just as much about the liberation of men and even affects the liberation of the rest of God's creation. The insights of women have to do with discovering our true humanity in the context of a right relationship with the rest of creation. They are erecting signposts pointing in the direction of how we can all live together respectfully in our world today.

Throughout this chapter the reader might have been wondering who are these women I have been referring to when I have used expressions like 'the voices of women today' or 'what women are writing and saying today'. Do I mean *all* women? Or if only *some* women, am I not already being discriminatory? Obviously, I do not mean just any woman who opens her mouth or picks up her pen. I have been referring to a growing number of women who are articulating something fundamental that would seem to lie deep in their experience precisely as women, even though as yet not all women are ready to own this experience. This 'something fundamental' has both a negative and positive side to it. The negative side is the denial of their full humanity as women that is ingrained in the structures of life in a whole variety of ways. The positive side is an increasing insight into the deeper meaning of being human that they are able to offer from their experience as women.

The authenticity of what they are saying would seem to be verified by the liberating effect it has on the lives and thinking of so many women, once they are really able to hear what these women are saying; and also by the parallel liberating effect it has on the lives and thinking of so many men as well. In some strange way it would seem that now at last in our age the time is ripe for these things to be said and acted upon. These women are inviting us all to be 'human' in a much richer way than we were ever able to imagine or think possible before. Obviously, I would not want to suggest that these women are infallible. That is the last thing they would want to claim for themselves. These women are struggling to articulate a new truth for our age; or rather, they are articulating an old truth whose transforming power we are now beginning to understand in a new way.

Articulating deep truths is always a struggle and getting it right involves a lot of trial and error. And this is all the more true when it also involves trying to interpret what is going on in life and how we should respond to the demands of practical living with all its dilemmas, conflicts of interests and uncertainty. That is all part of life and affects the Church itself just as much as it does these women. In fact, many of these women are themselves members of the Church. Sadly they feel they belong to a Church in which their voices precisely *as women* have been silenced. Others among them are not Christian or regard themselves as post-Christian. Their voices too must be listened to by the Church. Moreover, the Church must not listen to the voices of women merely with a view to passing some kind of definitive judgement as to what is acceptable and what is not acceptable in what they are saying. That would betray a mentality which believes that really the Church has nothing to learn from them, as though the Church no longer had need for a better understanding of the Good News. That is not Vatican II's vision of the Church and its relation to the Gospel:

The Church herself knows how richly she has profited by the history and development of humanity. Thanks to the experience of past ages, the progress of the sciences and the treasures hidden in the various forms of human culture, what it means to be human [my non-sexist translation of *ipsius hominis natura*] is more clearly revealed and new roads to truth are opened . . .

With the help of the Holy Spirit, it is the task of the entire People of God, especially pastors and theologians, to hear, distinguish, and interpret the many voices of our age, and to judge them in the light of the divine Word. In this way, revealed truth can always be more deeply penetrated, better understood, and set forth to greater advantage. (*Gaudium et Spes*, n. 44)

The voices of women we have been listening to in this chapter must surely merit a major inclusion among 'the many voices of our age' referred to above. Moreover, it would seem reasonable to conclude that women theologians have a unique role in 'hearing, distinguishing and interpreting' the voices of women. Hence, part of the message of Vatican II is that the Church must pay special attention today to what women theologians are saying and that it can only do this if women themselves fully participate in that process of listening and interpreting. In this decade of evangelization the Church is more than ever committed to doing this if it is to present to the world the Good News in all its fullness for today. I believe the following paraphrase captures the true sense of the last sentence of the above quotation as applied to this particular issue: 'Through the church's listening to women theologians as they hear, distinguish and interpret the voices of their sisters today, revealed truth can be more deeply penetrated, better understood, and set forth to greater advantage'.

This chapter has been an exercise in listening, based on a wide variety of women's writing relevant to moral theology and on conversations with many women involved in theological and pastoral issues. It has been an attempt to listen to what these women theologians are saying to us, men as well as women, as they point out to us the direction in which we need to be going if we are to live lives which are more fully and authentically human. I have not dared to attempt to voice the negative dimension of the oppression of women which has served to heighten their appreciation of what is so lacking in our current way of being human. That is best articulated by the voices of women themselves. Hence, I have left the reader to consult the many powerful presentations of women's multifaceted experience of the oppressiveness of patriarchy in its various forms, as found in society and in the Church down through the ages.

The words of an Irish women artist, Ailbhe Smyth, have made me very conscious of the danger of distortion in what I have attempted to do it this chapter:

> What women have to say, in whatever medium, is still liable to be transposed into the terms of the dominant male discourse — and denied in the process. 'What that woman who dares to speak really means is . . .', 'I know what that woman is really trying to say'. But they don't because they can't hear and don't want to share a space they have occupied for so long. ('Commonplaces, proper places' in *Strongholds: New Art From Ireland* (Tate Gallery Liverpool, 1991), p. 46)

When I first read those words I wondered whether this chapter was doomed to failure. However, in the end I decided to forge ahead. A book exploring the theme of diversity in moral thinking would be seriously incomplete without a serious attempt to listen to the voices of women as interpreted by their sisters who are theologians.

Chapter 6

THE CHRISTIANITY OF HUMAN MORALITY

In the course of this book we have examined a number of issues related to the question of disagreement on moral issues. We saw that the very possibility of disagreement was based on an underlying agreement that there is such a thing as human morality. This led us to explore the common foundations on which this human morality would seem to be based. We located these common foundations in the dignity of the human person and tried to probe the implications of this by examining the different dimensions of being human shared by all human persons. We acknowledged that what we share in common at this level does not imply that there should be exactly the same moral codes across the various cultures. Hughes reminded us that 'there will be as many acceptable moral codes as there are different coherent patterns of true beliefs' (cf. p. 20 above). In fact, our very diversity actually flows from what we share in common as human persons, particularly the fact that we are persons in history, social beings belonging to a particular culture and yet each of us unique and possessing creative freedom. We saw, too, that experience is an essential factor in the growth of our moral understanding. As well as learning from our mistakes we deepen our moral understanding both through our increased knowledge of ourselves and our world and also through having to tackle new situations.

The objection might be raised that all these issues are concerned with ordinary human morality. What is Christian about what I have written so far? That is the question I wish to address in this chapter. It is central to the whole theme of the book. I have left it to near the end not because I consider it unimportant but because I believe that its significance can only be grasped when we have faced the other issues treated in the rest of the book.

Christian morality: wise and loving living in the light of Christian revelation

I would not want to claim a Cana-like quality for this chapter, 'keeping the best wine to the end', as it were. Nevertheless, there is a feature of the Cana story which does strike me as very relevant. At Cana the water was turned into wine. My basic thesis in this chapter is that Christian revelation opens our eyes to the wonder of wise and loving human living. What seems to be the ordinary water of human morality is revealed to be the rich wine of Christian morality. In saying this, however, I am not suggesting that human morality is less precious (like water) and, through being lived by Christians, is turned into the wine of Christian morality. I would want to say far more than that.

Christian revelation enables us to see that wise and loving human living actually *is* Christian morality. It is living in conformity with the mind and heart of Christ who in his own person is 'the love of God made visible in our midst'. In other words, we are following a false trail if our search for Christian morality is directed towards trying to isolate some particular content of moral living which is specifically Christian. That is not where we should be looking. Admittedly, as an identifiable religious community, Christians may be faced with moral decisions specific to their religious affiliation and their Church's beliefs and practices (e.g. choosing a religious vocation, or participating in the liturgy). As a result of this, Christians within some Churches, as a distinct group with their own traditions, symbols, language and authority structures, will have developed moral positions on concrete issues (e.g. abortion) which tend to be identified with them, even though not exclusive to them. This is a perfectly natural, sociological phenomenon and requires no specific revelation to explain it. However, to identify Christian morality with these kinds of specific issues would be to impoverish it.

I would suggest that the term Christian morality, in its richest sense, means the light thrown on human moral living by Christian revelation. That light in no way downgrades wise and loving human living. Far from it! Christian revelation shows us that, whether we are Christians or not and whether we realize it or not, whenever we are engaged in wise and loving living, we are actually living out the love of God.

The love of God made visible in our midst

Jesus did not come to teach us new moral truths, hitherto hidden from the human family. In his own person he reveals to us that wise and loving human living is how the love of God is made incarnate within human life. In his own personal situation, part of wise and loving living involved challenging the unlove and unwisdom of his day. For Jesus, wise and loving living involved empowering the marginalized (those made 'unclean' through sin, sickness and/or social ostracism) who were demoralized by the person-diminishing rejection of them by those who claimed to speak with God's authority.

Such wise and loving living on the part of Jesus brought him into conflict with the unlove and unwisdom of the authorities and it was their opposition which finally brought about his death. The willingness of Jesus to remain faithful to his commitment to wise and loving living right to the end meant that his death was part of that freely chosen commitment. It was, in fact, the supreme expression of his wise and loving living. It expressed his love and forgiveness for those who were part of the web of his life. Through his love and forgiveness of them, Jesus expressed the love and forgiveness of God for the whole human family, personified in them.

Moreover, this supreme expression of wise and loving living constituted the human consummation of his commitment to his Father's will. His resurrection and ascension brought this revelation to completion. Jesus' wise and loving life and death might have seemed to have ended in failure. If the grave was the end of the story, Jesus' life would seem to have ended with an act of human folly rather than wisdom, an act of reckless and irresponsible love, regardless of the consequences. The resurrection and ascension put the final seal of transcendence on his this-worldly life of wise and loving living. His following the path of wise and loving living right to the final witness of his 'laying down his life for his friends' was both a fulfilment of his life ('It is accomplished') and an unveiling of the 'new creation'. In no way should it be seen as the cessation of his wise and loving living. It is simply the completion of his living out in time and space the way of life which can more truly be described as 'eternal life'. In the final analysis, wise and loving living is nothing less than our human participation in the very life of God. It is the work of God's creative spirit, poured into our hearts and fashioning the unique image of God each of us is called to be. It is what John's gospel would call 'knowing' God, with all the overtones of 'two-in-oneness' that that expression suggests. Wise and loving living even in this life is already 'eternal life', though here still in its embryonic form.

More than a model for wise and loving living

However, there is still something further to be said. What I have said in the above paragraphs could give the impression that the moral relevance of the Christian revelation lies in the fact that in Jesus God gave us a model for wise and loving human living. It could seem as though in Jesus God set his final seal of approval on wise and loving living as the form of human living which is in keeping with our being made in the image of God. And so Jesus has shown us the life of God translated into human terms and that reveals itself in wise and loving living.

All that is profoundly true, of course. Yet, left there, it would fail to do justice to the full richness of Christian revelation and its implications for Christian morality.

The Judeo-Christian revelation, culminating in the life, death and resurrection of Jesus, is more than God's offering us a moral example in the person of Jesus. The core of Christian revelation is that we are loved by God — all of us, each and every person who has ever lived, who is living now and who will live in the future. We are all members of God's family. God is 'our' Father (and Mother!).

This revelation does not contradict human reason. We can still feel humbled by our puny-ness and wonder at our grandeur. The more we get to know about our expanding universe, its immensity, and the mind-boggling process of evolution over millions of centuries — everything starting, we are told, from a mass about the size of a tennis ball — the more we become conscious of our insignificance as a part of the whole, an infinitesimal speck in the cosmos. Yet the more too we become conscious of the immense privilege, and responsibility, we share as belonging to the highest life-form emerging from the process of evolution. The 'anthropic principle' takes our breath away. This kind of consciousness enables us to look at ourselves and each other with awe; but it also makes us appreciate how transient and disposable we are in the whole process. It is a consciousness that can lead us to reverence and respect for human persons. Yet it is also a consciousness which could lead us towards a discriminatory morality based on a competitive, 'survival of the fittest' kind of attitude. This could flow from an awareness of our insignificance and disposability as individuals and perhaps also from an unconscious 'species-survival' mechanism at work in us.

Judeo-Christian revelation with its belief that God's personal love is offered to each individual and that together we all make up God's family, brothers and sisters of each other, confirms and deepens certain dimensions of our natural consciousness described above. It confirms and deepens our innate sense of awe, which had led us naturally to a reverence and respect for human persons; and it also confirms and deepens our sense that we are not just a collection of individuals but that there is a oneness uniting us all and that consequently our personal good cannot be divorced from the good of the whole human species and the rest of creation. Yet Christian revelation also challenges certain negative tendencies which might flow from our natural consciousness. It challenges any tendency to allow a recognition of personal dignity to develop into a socially destructive autonomous individualism; and it challenges any tendency of our sense of solidarity with each other to develop into any form of totalitarianism which would regard individual persons as disposable for the good of the whole.

There is a further element in Judeo-Christian revelation which is very relevant for our moral stance. This can be approached from two angles which might seem very different but which are in fact intimately related.

A foundational truth in Judeo-Christian revelation is that the whole of creation has its origin in God and that human beings in particular are made in the image of God; and all God's handiwork, ourselves included, is 'very good'. As we have seen in Chapter 4, this foundational truth can be misinterpreted in a fundamentalist sense and consequently can be understood as suggesting that whatever 'is' in nature constitutes 'the Maker's instructions' and so must be given absolute respect. This ignores the crucial fact that 'the Maker' has made us intelligent creatures and this very intelligence constitutes an essential dimension of our being which 'the Maker' has declared to be good. Hence, even within the metaphor of 'the Maker's instructions', we could say that 'the Maker's instructions' are that we should *live intelligently*. And, despite countless lapses resulting from human folly or ignorance, the human family has in fact tried to live intelligently down through the ages. Moreover, this intelligent living has led 'naturally' to the rise of civilization and the story of civilization continues through into our own day with all its 'artificial' adaptations of 'natural processes' found in modern developments in science and technology affecting so many areas of human life. Hence, as we have seen, it can be argued that these 'artificial' developments, provided they are in the service of wise and loving living in the human community, are completely in keeping with 'the

Maker's instructions', even though they may be far removed from what happens 'naturally'.

However, the unique 'goodness' of the human species lies not just in the fact that 'the Maker' has made us intelligent persons. We have also been made loving persons, having the inclination and capacity to relate to each other through the unifying power of love. This unifying power of love is embodied very specially in the sexual dimension of our being. It also links in with the social dimension of our being. As human persons we are essentially interdependent. Hence, it has ramifications also for social morality, where justice too can be spoken of in terms of the language of wise and loving social living.

Wise and loving living — made in the image of the trinitarian God

This interdependent dimension of our being is where the foundational truth of creation and our being made in the image of God merges with another major truth of Christian revelation. Jesus has revealed to us that the God in whose image we are made is a God whose being cannot adequately be expressed in human language simply in terms of *one* God. The God that Jesus reveals to us is certainly a God who is one. Jesus proclaims: 'I and the Father are one' and he prays that we might be one as he and the Father are one. But the God Jesus reveals is also a God whose oneness is not a oneness of aloneness or isolated individuality. The God of Jesus is a God whose oneness is actually the rich relational unity of Father and Son bound together by the personal love of the Spirit. In the comprehension-defying 'mystery' of this God we encounter a 'personal' being whose oneness, far from swallowing up relational diversity, actually lives by it.

To believe that we are made in the image of this God gives a new depth to what we mean when we say that as human persons we are essentially interdependent, a dimension of our being greatly emphasized by women theologians. It also makes us aware that when we are dealing with the dimensions of our embodiment which have a special bearing on our relational capacities (and this includes but extends far beyond our sexual faculties), we are on very hallowed ground. That is not to say that this ground is a 'no-go' area to which we must not apply our intelligence. It is saying rather that this is a dimension of human living which touches deeply on our dignity as human persons. Hence, we must be at our most intelligent in handling this dimension of our being. This is true in the field of sexual ethics, but surely it is equally true in all the other 'relational' fields such as politics, economics, communications and social ethics in general.

The vision of Christian morality coming through in all this is that wise and loving living is at the heart of how we respond to God's love for us. We love God by loving each other and by respecting ourselves. Aquinas was clearly working out of this vision when he stated that we only offend God insofar as we harm ourselves or other persons (cf. *Contra Gentiles*, III, n. 122). It is a vision which can be traced through the gospels right back into the Old Testament. In answer to the question put to him by the scribe as to which is the greatest of the commandments, Jesus gives an answer which combines the commandment found in Deuteronomy 6:4–5 with that in Leviticus 19:18: 'You shall love the Lord your God with all your heart, and with all your soul, and with all your mind. This is the great and first commandment. And a second is like it. You shall love your neighbour as yourself' (Matt 22:37–39, RSV translation). John Burnaby comments that the force of the word 'like' in this passage is to say that both commandments really mean the same thing (in John Macquarrie and James Childress (eds), *A New Dictionary of Christian Ethics* (SCM, 1986), p. 354). Karl Rahner expresses the unity of these two commandments very powerfully:

> There is no love for God that is not, in itself, already a love for neighbour; and love for God only comes to its own identity through its fulfilment in a love for neighbour. Only one who loves his or her neighbour can know who God actually is. And only one who ultimately loves God (whether he or she is reflexively aware of this or not is another matter) can manage unconditionally to abandon himself or herself to another person, and not make that person the means of his or her own self-assertion.
>
> . . . If we understand love of God and a brotherly/sisterly communion as two expressions denoting basically the same thing . . . then we may safely say that with a communion of brothers and sisters, in its necessary oneness with the love of God, we have expressed the single totality of the task of the whole human being and of Christianity. (*The Love of Jesus and the Love of Neighbour* (St Paul, 1983), pp. 71, 84)

This links in with the basic theme of this book, namely, that the human person's faith-response to God, whether he or she recognizes it or not, is expressed in our lives rather than in our credal affirmations. In a 1976 interview with Gerhard Ruis of the Vienna *Presse*, Rahner puts this very clearly:

> Wherever there is selfless love, wherever duties are carried out without hope of reward, wherever the incomprehensibility of death is calmly accepted, wherever people are good with no hope of reward, in all these instances the Spirit is experienced . . . The question whether they can define it as such or verbalize it may be important humanly speaking — for faith or theology — but in the end it is of secondary importance . . . Those who love totally and absolutely have already loved God and encountered the Spirit, whether they acknowledge it or not. (Paul Imhof and Hubert Biallowons (eds), *Karl Rahner in Dialogue: Conversations and Interviews 1965–1982* (New York: Crossroad, 1986), pp. 142–3)

The Church as teacher of morality

Where does the teaching authority of the Church fit into this picture? The teaching role of the Church is primarily to announce the Good News of God's love for all men and women. Most of the first section of this chapter has pointed out how this Good News provides the foundation for what we mean by Christian morality. Obviously, then, the teaching authority of the Church, in its primary role of announcing the Good News, is playing a crucial role with regard to the vision of Christian morality I have been putting forward. Without the basic truths of our Christian revelation wise and loving human living, though still a way of life to be admired and followed, would not be fully appreciated as having the awesome meaning and significance we were exploring earlier.

If we believe that morality, that is, how we respond to each other as human persons, matters to God — and I have argued that that belief provides the grounding of Christian morality — then this is a truth that the Church has the duty to proclaim, in season and out of season. The Church would be untrue to its role as teacher if it were to give the impression that the relevance of the Gospel stopped at the church door and that the Christian faith was principally about public liturgy and private prayer and devotions. To express its concern for justice and the dignity of human persons is certainly within the Church's sphere of competence. The Church would be neglecting its mission if it failed to proclaim as powerfully as it can that morality matters to God.

Is that all the Church has the competence and authority to say? I would prefer to turn the question the other way round. Could the Church credibly proclaim that morality matters to God and then take no interest in matters of morality? In proclaiming that morality matters to God, the Church is not proclaiming some abstract truth. To say that morality matters to God is simply a shorthand way of saying that how men and women behave towards each other, personally and collectively, matters to God, as does the way they treat the rest of God's creation. In other words, saying that morality matters to God is part of saying that human persons matter to God, as does the rest of creation.

To proclaim this truth with any credibility, the Church must proclaim it with reference to people today. In other words, the Church must proclaim it with concern for the way people are treating themselves, each other and the rest of God's creation at the present time. The object of such proclamation is to help people live as wisely and lovingly as possible in our modern world. It goes without saying, of course, that such proclamation will ring very hollow if the Church is not actively involved in bringing about such wise and loving living and if the Church is not committed to opposing the personal and systematic or structural factors which work against the possibility of such wise and loving living.

Has the Church any special competence in judging what exactly is wise and loving living in particular areas of life, a competence which would enable it to speak with authority on such matters?

At one level, the fact that the core truths of the Christian faith have an impact on the way we understand the human person can give the Church the competence to speak with special authority on certain matters. For instance, there is a contradiction between these core truths and any moral system which holds that the human person is a totally independent individual, having no responsibility whatsoever for his or her fellow human beings. Presumably no serious-minded person would propound such an absurd position which is so completely at odds with reality as we know it. Interdependence, as we have seen, is a fact of life. Nevertheless, less extreme forms of individualism are put forward and accepted as plausible forms of personal or social morality. If such ideologies hold sway in society, contradicting the reality of our human interdependence, the Church is competent to judge that they are inhuman and so irreconcilable with the Christian message. Such a judgement will obviously necessitate a careful analysis of the precise position being criticized. Given this, such a judgement will draw its basic insight from the core truths of Christian revelation. I would like to think that perhaps these core truths of Christian revelation equip the Church with antennae which are particularly sensitive to interpretations of the human person which threaten to be dehumanizing through an over-individualistic tendency.

There is also a contradiction between the core truths of our faith and any moral system which reduces the human person to a mere part in the social collectivity without any inviolable intrinsic dignity or worth. Once again, I would like to think that Christian revelation equips the Church with antennae which are especially sensitive to any tendency to move in the direction of totalitarianism or even person-violating discrimination on grounds of colour, race, sex or creed. Perhaps Christian antennae would also send out warning signals in the face of life-styles based on some kind of determinist interpretation of life, as for instance has been alleged to be true of some New Age thinking.

However, in relation to all that I have written above, I would want to insist that 'the Church' should not be interpreted as referring merely to its office-holders. There is no reason to presume that their antennae will be any more sensitive than those of other committed Christians.

I believe that to the extent that it is living in conformity with the Gospel it preaches, the Church can claim special competence in both these directions. Sadly, history shows that the sinfulness of the Church has meant that at times it has shown itself incompetent in both these directions. Nevertheless, as noted in Chapter 1, part of the driving force behind Vatican II was a desire on the part of the Church to renew itself and so regain any competence it had lost in these areas. The Council's emphasis on reading the signs of the times was perhaps an exercise in re-sensitizing its antennae. Moreover, if *Gaudium et Spes* is anything to go by, this re-sensitization process was very effective within the Council itself. And it did not end with the Council. It has gradually been percolating through the rest of the Church, clearly more successfully in some areas than in others. Certainly the decisions of the Latin American Church at Medellín in 1968 were a result of this post-conciliar process.

Another possible ground for special competence in discerning what is wise and loving living in particular areas of life lies in the sacramental nature of the Church. The Vatican II Constitution on the Church defined the Church as follows: 'By her relationship with

Christ, the church is a kind of sacrament or sign of intimate union with God, and of the unity of all humankind. She is also an instrument for the achievement of such union and unity' (n. 1). Of course, this definition of the Church applies to the whole People of God. Hence, its application should not be seen as principally, and certainly not solely, applied to the Church precisely as institution. As Avery Dulles has pointed out, the Church as institution is only one model of the Church and it has a very limited validity. It is the whole Church precisely as the People of God who have a special competence in the area of wise and loving living. They are the sacrament of our unity with God and with each other precisely through their wise and loving living.

Naturally, I am not suggesting that they have an exclusive or sole claim to competence with regard to wise and loving living. From before the dawn of history the real story of humankind is that of the wise and loving living of men and women of all faiths and none, a story shot through with ambiguity, tragedy and sin. Yet, despite that, it is the Spirit-filled story of all God's family. However, I do believe that Christians have their own special claim to competence in wise and loving living. They are a group of people who, since the time of Christ, have believed that wise and loving living matters to God and so, as a group, despite all their sinfulness, inadequacy and ignorance, they have tried to live wisely and lovingly as best they know how. This does not make them infallible judges of wise and loving living. It does suggest that they have a right to be heard. They can speak with the authority of their experience. Clearly, they have not been alone in this venture of trying to live wisely and lovingly. That has been a common task shared by the whole human family.

I suspect that history would not bear me out if I tried to claim that Christians have led the field in all the movements down through the ages which have furthered the cause of the dignity of the human person and the social reforms needed to safeguard and respect that dignity. Nevertheless, I suspect that Christians would score fairly highly in the human rights and reform stakes. After all, it is not necessary to believe that the People of God is all-wise and all-loving in order to argue that it has a wealth of wise and loving living to share with the human family. And this empowers it to speak with its own specific authority. It could even be said that an important part of what it has to share is drawn from its experience of sin and failure, an experience turned into something positive and fruitful through its belief in the loving forgiveness of God.

Is there anything distinctive about Christian morality?

Have Christians anything to say about wise and loving living which is distinctive and which cannot be said by other people who are also concerned about wise and loving living?

This is a topic which has been the subject of lively debate among moral theologians in recent years. There is no disagreement about the fact that the core truths of Christian revelation provide the basic foundation for Christian morality. Neither is there any disagreement that in the religious field (e.g. vocation to the religious life, obligations regarding Christian liturgy, prayer etc.) there are moral demands which are special to Christians.

That measure of agreement being accepted, the debate focuses more particularly on whether the Christian faith gives its adherents any kind of distinctive or even privileged insight when it comes to the practical problems of moral living.

Our world-view is bound to influence our whole approach to life. Moreover, our world-view is not simply something that we work out from scratch for ourselves. It results from our personal inter-action with a whole series of interlocking influences, cultural, religious, historical, familial etc. This is true for us as Christians too. Furthermore, our world-view precisely as Christian is not just a series of ideas or abstract truths handed on to us. It is bound up with a belief in God's saving action in history, culminating in the life, death and resurrection of Jesus, and continuing down through the centuries in the Spirit-inspired life and memory of the Church, as we listen again to our Judeo-Christian narratives and stories and interpret life through a liturgy rich in symbols. This world-view, as we have seen already in this chapter, has important implications for the way we view persons and life itself, especially those dimensions of human life in which our interdependence is most in evidence. Vincent MacNamara puts this well when he writes:

> While much of secular moral literature is based on concepts of interest and desires, on one's right to a fair share of the available goods . . . the Bible tells us that we are to seek the interests of others and not our own, that we are to give to everyone who asks, wash one another's feet, forgive enemies, be prepared to lay down our lives for the neighbour. This curious asymmetry in relationships seems to be the logic of a faith that has stories about the forgiving love of God for us, about a Saviour who died for us when we were yet sinners, about the final and total meaning of our lives.

There is talk in Christianity too about bearing the cross . . . Moral literature generally seems to envisage situations of logic and clarity in which we are dealing with perfectly reasonable people. But we live in a world in which justice will not be done, in which rights will not be allowed, in which goodness will not be rewarded, in which evil prospers. A fair slice of life is about injustice and about situations which have injustice written into them. We must struggle for justice for ourselves and others, but in situations where we do not or are not likely to obtain it there must also be a Christian response: it cannot be a response that is divorced from the stories and symbols that are the very stuff of Christianity. (*The Truth in Love* (Gill and Macmillan, 1988), pp. 57–8)

MacNamara reminds us, too, that central to the Christian world-view is the belief that 'knowledge of God, awareness of him, friendship with him' is the supreme good. As he puts it, attention to this 'might well modify one's attitude to goods which a non-believer regards as important'. As an example of this he instances celibacy for the sake of the kingdom. He also points out that Christian tradition also believes in such values as detachment and trust, poverty of life and spirit, bearing one's cross. He admits that these prominent features of the Christian world-view could not be classified as concrete norms: 'They do not and are not meant to tell us exactly what to do. They are not precise directives but thrusts for living that grow out of how one regards oneself and one's world in Christ' (p. 58). His words here are reminiscent of how C. H. Dodd describes the law of Christ: 'It is an obligation to reproduce in human action the *quality* and the *direction* of the act of God by which we are saved' (*Gospel and Law* (Cambridge University Press, 1951), p. 71).

Morality is not just about human actions, and certainly it is not just about actions divorced from the person who is doing the action. Morality must be thought of primarily in terms of persons. Hence, why a person does an action is of major importance. A full answer to that 'Why' cannot be found in the immediate end that the agent has in view. It also touches the deeper reasons which motivate a person. As we have seen, our Christian faith deepens the reasons which motivate our wise and loving living. Moreover, since morality is primarily about persons, it is also about who we are. It is about personal character and virtue, as Aristotle and Aquinas recognized so clearly centuries ago. When morality is understood in this sense, it can hardly be denied that there is such a thing as a specific Christian morality. After all, for the very same reason there is also a specific Jewish, or Muslim, or Hindu morality!

Of course, the world-view of the persons in whose lives this specific Christian morality is found is necessarily also shaped by the cultural–historical influences of their day. A pure distilled Christian moral vision, unaffected by cultural and historical influences, does not exist. Hence, any attempt to isolate what is specific about Christian morality is, in a sense, doomed to failure. Christian morality only exists in Christian persons, who necessarily are persons of their culture and history. It is as unrealistic to try to isolate 'pure Christian morality' as it is to deny its reality enfleshed in the minds and hearts of individual Christians, saints and sinners.

Mention of sinners reminds us that a truth of our Christian faith which has far-reaching implications for wise and loving living is our belief in the gratuitous forgiveness of God offered to all men and women. MacNamara commented on this in the passage quoted above when he spoke of the 'curious asymmetry in relationships' which seems to be 'the logic of a faith that has stories about the forgiving love of God for us, about a Saviour who died for us when we were yet sinners'. This leads into the theme of our next chapter. Although it will be looking at sin, that chapter will, in reality, be a continuation of our consideration of the Christian dimension of human morality. For the Christian the very word 'sin' is a theological term. It can only be understood against the positive, hope-filled backcloth of God's forgiving love. Jesus himself said that he had come to call sinners. Christianity interprets those words in an inclusive sense. Our very interdependence as human persons makes us sharers in each other's sinfulness. By owning that co-sinfulness each time we come together as a eucharistic community, representing the whole human family, we present our credentials as human persons in the face of the God of forgiveness. We are creatures utterly dependent on God who is inviting us from the depths of our being to let our real humanity be liberated through a process of healing, growth and final fulfilment.

Chapter 7

THE INHUMANITY OF SIN
AND THE HUMANITY OF FORGIVENESS

Sin reconsidered

If there was one issue above all on which Jesus disagreed radically with the Jewish leaders it was that of forgiveness. They were strong on sin, but weak on forgiveness. Jesus recognized the presence of sin in people's lives but his approach to it was one of healing rather than condemnation. This disagreement touches the very roots of moral theology. It is not a disagreement about what precise actions should be considered to be wrong or inhuman. That is the kind of disagreement we concentrated on earlier in this book. Disagreement about forgiveness, however, is quite different from that. It is rather a disagreement about the relationship between God and sinners — which includes all of us. At root, it is a disagreement about what kind of God we believe in and how this God relates to human beings and the rest of creation.

Consequently, its principal focus is not on specific human actions. God's forgiveness is directed towards the person who is the source of these inhuman actions. The parable of the prodigal son (or, to be more accurate, the parable of the two sons) makes it clear that God is not looking for retribution. His chief concern is for the healing of the sinner. He wants him to come to life again. It is clear that life in this case is not just a matter of individual health and prosperity. It is also about loving relationships. Hence, the sadness of the father over the unloving intransigence of his elder son. The tableau of the final judgement broadens this vision still further and insists that we are blind to what life is about if we ignore the social dimensions of human living. Our neighbours in need are an essential dimension of our own personal identity as human beings.

True to the gospels, the Catholic Church has always approached sin from the angle of forgiveness. This is very healthy. However, the healing power of this forgiveness became somewhat obscured through the application of the 'criminal tribunal' model to the sacrament of forgiveness. The name that was commonly used to refer to this sacrament, Confession, gave the game away. We approached the judgement seat of the tribunal of Penance and, convicted by our own confession, pleaded guilty before the priest, whose role was seen as that of judge. For his part the priest saw a major part of his role as judging how guilty this self-confessing party actually was. Like any wise judge he would be alert to the possibility of deception, including self-deception, and he would also look out for indications of scrupulosity which would impute guilt where there was none. Once the priest-judge had reached his verdict about the real guilt of the person, he could begin to explore whether he was justified in pronouncing a juridical absolution of this guilt. That necessitated his having moral certainty that the person was genuinely repentant for the sins confessed and was firmly determined to avoid them for the future. This latter require-ment posed problems since often both the guilty party and the priest-judge knew that it was more than likely that there would be a repetition of the offence. Experience showed that frequently even a very genuine firm purpose of amendment failed to deliver the goods.

The trouble about using this 'criminal tribunal' model in our approach to sin is that it cannot properly accommodate the Gospel emphasis on the healing dimension of forgiveness. The focus tends to be on sin as something we do. It is an offence we have committed and forgiveness is rather like having a parking-ticket cancelled. This separates too drastically what we do from ourselves as the source of our actions. As Jesus insisted, our sins come from within us. They are the bad fruits of our sinfulness.

To be fair to the 'criminal tribunal' approach, a major part of the 'judgemental' role of the priest was directed towards discerning just how far what we had done was in fact due to our personal fault. The priest-judge did not simply have to decide whether an 'offence' had been committed. He also had to examine whether we actually knew that what we had done was an offence and whether we had acted with sufficient freedom to make us personally responsible for the offence.

That is fine as far as it goes. However, it seems to assume that the essence of sin lies in 'bad will'. This is coming close to saying that our intention is all that matters. Provided we meant well there was no sin. That seems to present a rather disembodied approach to sin. It ignores the fact that inhumanity, not simply 'bad will', lies at the heart of sin; and inhumanity, like humanity, is a multi-dimensional reality. In fact, if we wanted to examine what is meant by the inhumanity of sin in very down-to-earth terms, we would need to look at the various ways in which the behaviour of individuals and groups runs counter to any of the eight dimensions of being a human person which we examined in Chapter 3.

Moreover, seeing sin in terms of inhumanity helps to focus our attention more on the mystery of the presence of evil in our world. Experience brings home to us how much our world, our own lives and our very selves are influenced by this presence of evil. We also know from experience that we are not only the victims of evil outside of us; we ourselves are also perpetrators of evil. This multi-faced mystery of evil raises deep human questions which the great myths of our world try to grapple with. When the practice of the sacrament of reconciliation cuts its moorings from the deep mystery of evil in us and in our world, it becomes trivialized and can itself even become a dehumanizing experience. There may be a value in 'confessions of devotion' properly understood. There is little or no value in confessions which are more to do with a fear-ridden, religious immaturity than with any true sense of sin and belief in a loving and forgiving God.

Victims of sin

As mentioned already, Christianity sees sin against the backcloth of forgiveness. Sin for the Christian is a theological word. It suggests the hope of forgiveness and healing. In line with this focus, before we look at ourselves as people who commit sin, we need first to see how far we ourselves are the victims of sin. This is important. It touches on the mystery that the Christian faith is grappling with in its teaching on original sin.

In his book *Let This Mind Be in You* (Darton, Longman & Todd, 1985), chapters 24 to 26, Sebastian Moore suggests that Christian teaching on original sin is really about the unmasking of a lie. This lie consists in the bad self-image which, deep down, seems to be ingrained in all of us as human persons and which we accept as true and unchangeable. Moore's explanation of this bad self-image need not detain us here. Suffice it to say that he seems to link it to the impossibility of our experiencing any totally satisfying human fulfilment for the desire to be loved and to love completely as persons. This desire, in which, according to Moore, our very sexuality is grounded, is ultimately our yearning for God. Its non-fulfilment creates a deep inner loneliness in us. Unrelieved, this loneliness is the root of all human evil. It turns us in on ourselves, as we try to achieve a dehumanizing self-sufficiency and thus deny our fundamental interdependence. The internalization of this lie is like a cancer, destroying any possibility of the development of any true sense of self-worth in us. Sebastian Moore points out that a further twist in this tragedy is that sometimes religious people present the 'lie' as being the 'truth' of the Christian teaching on original sin:

> [Original sin] has managed to perform a brilliant trick or sleight-of-hand. It has persuaded religious people that the comment, 'And that's just the way it is,' is the voice of God. They say, 'You can't change human nature because of original sin.' That's absolutely true. But what it means is, 'Human nature is prevented from changing by original sin, *which is the belief that human nature cannot be changed.*'
>
> What has happened is that the *voice* of original sin, 'That's just the way it is,' has masqueraded as the *doctrine* of original sin. With the disastrous consequence that preaching the doctrine of original sin is reinforcing the voice of original sin. (p. 85)

The Christian faith, in whose truth we are baptized, offers us healing from this cancer by unmasking the lie of original sin. Jesus in his own person is the truth that sets us free. He is the love of God made visible in our midst. Not only does he affirm that we are people of dignity and worth by reminding us that we are actually made in the image of God and loved by him. He even takes on board the evil that is ingrained in us by the lie of original sin and liberates us from it. In his passion and death he endures in his own person the very worst that human self-hatred and hatred of others can inflict. By enduring this with forgiveness he gives the lie to any notion of a God of stern retribution and reveals to us a God of forgiveness and healing. As Moore himself writes: 'The essential effect of sin — the crucified — is, identically, the healing. What sin ultimately is, is seen in the crucified' (*The Crucified Is No Stranger* (Darton, Longman & Todd, 1977), pp. 8–9).

The lie which is referred to by the powerful metaphor of original sin is not an invention of the Church. It touches on something which seems to be universally present in human experience. All humankind seems to be radically flawed by the acceptance of this untruth. Our Christian metaphor uses the term 'original' because the origin of this untruth seems to be 'rooted' in some aspect of our human condition rather than in something done by our first ancestors, though that is one interpretation often given to the teaching on original sin. The term 'sin' is used, against the backcloth of the Adamic myth, to remind us that this untruth, though universal, is not natural. It is not an essential dimension of the human condition. It is not part of God's work of creation. Sin does not originate in God. The 'lie' of original sin consists in claiming that it is an essential dimension of being human. Jesus was not a party to that lie. The saving truth he brought us exposed the falsity of that lie.

The trouble with this lie is that it wounds our capacity to love and respect ourselves and each other. We lack a personal security rooted in a belief in our own self-worth. This means that our experience of each other carries a dimension of threat as well as gift. Summarizing the thought of Moore on this point, Vernon Gregson writes: 'We are caught between the memory, if it can be spoken of as such, of our unconscious union with the cosmos, a union which as a species we have left behind in becoming self-conscious and therefore human, and our desire for a now conscious union with all and with the All, which we can only long for either as gift or as achievement' (in Timothy Fallon and Philip Boo Riley (eds), *Religion in Context: Recent Studies in Lonergan* (University of America Press, 1988), pp. 127–8).

This ambiguity has a pre-history for each of us since the web of relationships we are born into already carries the wounds of this ambiguity. That is equally true of all the groups, societies and communities which we enter into throughout the journey of our lives — including the Christian community too. We are both inheritors of grace and victims of sin at the same time.

By 'victims of sin' I mean that as we gradually come to self-awareness, we discover that we are wounded human persons, due to the influence of others and our own reaction to their influence. Our woundedness can touch all the eight dimensions of being a person that we examined in Chapter 3. The dawning of this self-understanding offers us the 'God-given' opportunity for entering into the life-long process of personal healing and growth. This is the dimension of life which we should be celebrating symbolically in the sacrament of reconciliation. Accepting as gift the wounded person we discover ourselves to be, we can try to become as fully human as we can within our limitations. In trying, however haltingly, to live positively in this way we are casting our vote in favour of life. In the process our fundamental option is taking shape. This is exposing the lie of original sin. It is beginning to believe in myself.

It opens the way to accepting myself as gift from God. It enables me to appreciate my unique giftedness and so see myself as a personal vocation from God. God is inviting me to use my gifts creatively so that I can image his goodness in an unrepeatable way in human history.

Such a lofty vocation does not mean that I do not remain a 'victim of sin'. My woundedness will show in all sorts of ways. And since it is 'my' woundedness, there will be some of me in the inhumanity that shows through. It will not be the 'real' me, the 'me' I want to be if God's Kingdom is to come in my life. Nevertheless, it really will be me. I cannot disown this side of myself. If I do, I will never achieve the healing this side of me needs — and, deep down, longs for.

Felix culpa (happy fault) — the paradox of my sinfulness

There is a kind of paradox at play here. In one sense, to the extent that I let my woundedness get the upper hand, to that extent I am being less than human in myself and I will be relating inhumanly to other people. After all, sin is dehumanizing. Yet in another sense, the very experience of my woundedness and the inhumanity it brings into my life and that of others is the very stuff out of which repentance and healing is fashioned. It is a classic example of *felix culpa*. To experience my need for healing and forgiveness is an inescapable stage in the process of being healed and forgiven. Jesus said he did not come to call the just but sinners. He insisted that it was the sick, not the healthy, who need a doctor. If we are to believe in a Saviour, we need to experience our own need of salvation.

This book is based on the belief that God wants us to be as fully human as we can. I was almost going to add 'within our own personal and unique limitations' but that would merely be stating the obvious. There is no other way any of us can be fully human except within our own personal and unique limitations. Some of the women theologians referred to in Chapter 5 have helped us become more conscious that our limitations are actually our opportunities. They provide the raw material with which, in God's providence, each of us has to work.

Gabriel Daly, in his book *Creation and Redemption* (Gill and Macmillan, 1988), offers an evolutionist interpretation of 'original sin'. Though differing somewhat from Moore's interpretation, in some ways it complements it. Daly looks at the long and slow development of *homo sapiens* from the animal world which leads to the stage of 'hominization' where for the first time a creature becomes 'conscious of itself'. With this self-consciousness, bringing freedom of choice with it, sin becomes part of the story of evolving humanity. For Daly original sin is linked to the feeling of alienation that human beings experience as they undergo this slow process of becoming human. It is the tension between what they have in common with the animal world (the instinct for self-preservation, survival of the fittest, etc.) and what makes them different from other animals (the struggle to love in a disinterested way, the power of human reasoning, etc.). In the Adamic myth, according to Paul Ricoeur, Adam is not some original Superman: he is an archetypal representative of every human person. His condition is the condition of all of us. Original sin expresses the dark underside of our graced humanity and our graced world. Human maturity, as with other forms of slow evolution, is a goal to be achieved through trial and error, chance and necessity. It is not a state of original perfection which has been lost. This is not too dissimilar to the thinking of third-century Irenaeus, with his view of Adam and Eve as immature human beings and the human race gradually growing up towards Christ. This links in with his oft-quoted statement which could, in fact, serve as an alternative title for this book: 'The glory of God is the human person fully alive' (*Gloria Dei vivens homo*: *Adversus haereses*, IV, 20, 7).

Daly's interpretation prompts the thought that perhaps we should not see the 'truly human' as the 'starting-point' for what we regard as moral behaviour, a kind of bottom line, under which anything less is seen to be below par. Perhaps it would be better to see it more as the goal that lies ahead. This would mean that any partial realization of the 'truly human' in our lives would be seen as an achievement *en route*. This would make us see the material presented in Chapter 3 in a new light. The description of the eight dimensions of being human given there would be seen as an outline of what being human involves *insofar as we can envisage it at this stage of the journey*. In other words, this is the way ahead insofar as we can see it at present. Even so we are still a bit like a party of children on a school outing — most keeping more or less to the route, though at differing speeds, some straggling by the way and some wandering far away from the trail. We are a mixed bag of struggling humanity, trying to keep going but constantly tempted to give up and either go back or at least pitch camp where we are. What Daly is saying encourages us not to lose heart. Ahead of us lie possibilities of 'being truly human' which at present we can hardly imagine or can see only as a shadowy dream of an unattainable future.

Seen in this light, the healing we need would be the empowerment to leave behind the less-than-human in us. In other words, this healing would consist in the help we need to move beyond the lower level of being human we have reached and progress to a higher level of being human. For Daly, the basic insight involved in the notion of original sin is that 'to be human is to need redemption'. The redemption we need is precisely the empowerment described above. For Daly, therefore, sin would largely consist in our being content to remain where we are. This would be tantamount to refusing the invitation to play our part in the human family's journey towards becoming more 'truly human'. Seeing sin from this angle, we can understand why Bernard Lonergan, remarking on the unintelligibility of basic sin, says that it is 'not an event' and even describes it as 'failure of occurrence' (*Insight* (Longman, Green & Co., 1958), p. 667). It is a failure to be reasonable. As Vernon Gregson puts it: 'We crucify the resources of life, resources with which we might have created not only ourselves but a world with others to the praise of God' (in Timothy Fallon and Philip Boo Riley (eds), *Religion in Context*, p. 136).

Against this backcloth Daly looks at the demonic within us which he sees as being present in 'aggression, jealousy, possessive love, hatred, vengeance, fear, and a host of other primal emotions which can destroy us and our interhuman relationships if we do not name these emotions and "come to terms" with them' (p. 146). For him, these potentially destructive emotions 'are also the raw materials of holiness'. He goes on to say: 'We would not be human without the very forces which can destroy us'.

Daly's approach is somewhat similar to the interpretation of sin given by Jacques Pohier (cf. 'What purpose does sin serve?', *Theology Digest* (1978), pp. 24–8). He too sees the existence of sin as not being due to some original fall of our first ancestors but simply as flowing from the contingency and fallibility involved in being human:

> Is man a sinner because Adam was one and has thus made man other than what he should be? Or is man a sinner simply because he is a man? If the latter, the reason why man is a sinner is not sin but the fact that

man is man. Is it not natural for a being whose liberty is not God's, a being for whom contingency is natural, to be a sinner? If so, isn't it equivocal to say that God did not want man's nature to be fallible and that a striking consequence of his grace is to dispense us from our nature? God does not save man by making him impeccable but by pardoning sin. Salvation consists in God's becoming a God-with-us who are sinful and contingent. (p. 27 — the sexist language is that of his *Theology Digest* abstracter!)

It is not surprising, therefore, that Pohier speaks of the demonic in us in much the same way as does Daly: 'Violence and aggression [are seen] not only as natural and normal elements of life, but even as something positive, indispensable for life itself . . . Man's conflictual character is part of his psychic make-up and indispensable for his functioning' (*Creation and Redemption*, p. 146).

The approach of Daly and Pohier is not unconnected with the point I was emphasizing a little earlier. The precise way I am a 'victim of sin' will affect the way in which I grow into being more human. For instance, it should give me a sensitivity and compassion for those who are victims of sin in a similar way to myself and it should also make me appreciate the suffering caused by the inhumanity of sin in this particular dimension of human living.

Not a perfectionist ethic

To believe that God wants us to be as fully human as we can is not to believe in a perfectionist ethic, though, unfortunately, Roman Catholic moral teaching is sometimes interpreted in this way. The trouble with a perfectionist ethic is that it cannot cope with failure. Impossible standards merely aggravate the negativity of feeling I have failed. That opens the door to believing I am a failure. This plays right into the hands of the lie of original sin. To believe myself to be a failure is to believe myself to be no good. A perfectionist ethic merely confirms the negativity of failure. It implicitly says that original sin is not a lie but is true — I am hopeless, beyond all hope!

Christianity with its focus on its crucified–risen Lord is open to the possibility that there can be a positive side to failure. The 'rock bottom' experience can be the tomb out of which we can rise to new life. Moore expresses this mystery very succinctly: 'This is the ultimate mystery of us: that even our evil, even our tendency against wholeness, exposes us to the love of God' (*The Crucified Is No Stranger*, p. 55). As Moore is hinting, the conversion potentiality latent in such a 'rock-bottom' experience needs a positive climate, if it is to come to life. In a famous and very powerful sermon Paul Tillich brings this out when he portrays the person at rock bottom hearing the liberating words 'You are accepted'. This has the opposite effect to that of a perfectionist ethic. It generates the belief 'I am loved. Victim of sin and perpetrator of sin, though I am, I am accepted and loved by God.' To believe this is to believe I am a person of dignity and worth. And to believe that is to open myself to hearing and accepting the invitation 'Become who you are'. This is light years away from the crippling message 'You are a failure, you are beyond all hope'.

If sin should be seen in terms of inhumanity, it would follow that forgiveness should be seen in terms of healing. Of course, remembering that there are various dimensions to be human is a safeguard against developing a notion of healing based on a model of perfect health. Otherwise, we would be straight back to another version of the perfectionist ethic. As we saw in Chapter 3, among the essential dimensions of my humanity are my historicity and my personal uniqueness. Taken in combination these two dimensions are a reminder that my personal woundedness will have a history to it and will be unique to me. Likewise it will take time to heal and the healing when it occurs will be unique to me. Moreover, the scars resulting from it and the permanent disability it may leave me with will all be part of me. Dorothee Sölle makes the comment: 'I have noticed that people with faith all walk round with a limp!' (see below, p. 136). In other words, the scars of our healed woundedness will show. Each of us will bear our own unique scars. Like the glorious wounds of Jesus they will enhance our individual humanity.

Of course, we need to be careful we do not romanticize sin. Acknowledging the inhumanity of sin helps to remind us that there is nothing attractive about the various ways in which each of us is a 'victim of sin'. After all, these are ways in which our true humanity has failed to develop or has even become warped and distorted. There is nothing attractive about a deep lack of confidence and trust that leads a person to keep everyone at bay and refuse to love or be loved. Neither is there anything attractive about an acquisitiveness based on a lack of security that leads a person to seek attention by accumulating possessions, regardless of how much other persons might be hurt or impoverished in the process. The different ways in which we are victims of sin are the ways in which we ourselves, until we gradually become healed, will continue to wreak havoc around us and play our part in continuing the saga of reproducing other victims of sin, made in our own image and likeness.

Perpetrators of sin

What about the transition from being a victim of sin to being a perpetrator of sin? I have suggested already that the growing awareness of myself as a victim of sin can be the first stage in a life-long healing process. However, suppose this opportunity is not accepted. It is here that we begin to touch on the heart of the mystery of personal sin. Even here inhumanity continues to be appropriate language to use. Not to accept the invitation to enter into this healing process is implicitly to say that I prefer to live my life out of the inhumanity of my woundedness. This is to expose myself to the danger of this inhumanity spreading to other dimensions of my life and person. It is to refuse to accept the gift of the various dimensions of my being a human person that we examined in Chapter 3. It is to opt instead for my own reduced version of reality. Such a choice implicitly refuses my own unique personal giftedness. I feel threatened by the interdependence of human life and so I seek security not in the richness of my multi-dimensional humanity but in a dehumanized individualism which ultimately can only lead to loneliness, unhappiness and personal disintegration. In a sense, all sin is reality evasion. It is a refusal to continue the process of becoming our true selves. It is interesting to note in this connection that the Hebrew word for sin literally means 'to miss the target'.

The word 'sin' has more than one meaning. In examining these meanings I am working on the assumption that 'inhumanity' is the connecting link between them.

Although strictly speaking the terms 'wrong' or 'evil' are more accurate, sometimes the word 'sin' is used to describe human actions which are violations of the dignity of the human person and which contradict the kind of life needed if this dignity is to be properly respected. So murder, adultery, stealing, lying, etc. are said to be sinful. In this first usage the word 'sin' or 'sinful' is being used as shorthand for 'in violation of the dignity of human persons'. As we have seen already in our discussion of moral prohibitions, there is room for disagreement as to what precisely constitutes an action coming under one of these headings. This disagreement can be at a general level — how do we define 'murder' etc.?; or it can be at a particular level — does this particular action or kind of action fall within this definition? Some violations of human dignity are far more serious than others. Acknowledgement of this fact lay behind the distinction between light and grave matter which was commonplace in Roman Catholic manuals of moral theology.

This first way of speaking of sin is not without theological significance. How the members of the human family treat each other is not a matter of indifference to God. Whatever violates the dignity of human persons can in a very real sense be contrary to the will of God. That is why moral theologians are dissatisfied with an approach to sin found in some of the moral theology manuals which seemed to imply that all that mattered to God was whether we were personally guilty or not. It was as though God could only be offended by what went on in the depths of our being and was completely unconcerned as to whether human beings were causing each other to suffer or not. In an article in *The Way* I criticized that approach as follows:

> It bred an attitude which I can only call 'irresponsibility towards life'. It failed to see how much this life matters in the eyes of God. It almost reduced our present life to being a kind of waiting-room for eternity, a supporting feature before the main film. The emphasis was on my personal immunity from guilt, my integrity. As long as my conscience was clear, I did not need to worry.
>
> This life matters enormously to God. And above all, how human persons are treated is of paramount importance to God . . . If God really loves people and wants them to love and respect each other, it matters enormously to God how we treat each other and how we manage the world and universe that we share as our communal home. God is not an impartial and uninvolved judge passing guilty or not-guilty verdicts on people. God is a committed and deeply involved lover to whom the dignity and happiness of each of us is of crucial importance.
>
> A lover is a very vulnerable person since he or she suffers in and through the sufferings of the beloved. In freely creating humankind out of love, God has made himself completely vulnerable. ('Towards an adult conscience', *The Way* (1985), pp. 288–9)

The tears and anger of Jesus were not prompted solely by the disbelief of people. They were also in response to the suffering of people and the inhumanity of the way they were being treated. This suggests that the first meaning of sin, although not the basic meaning, is still very central.

If sin in this first sense is a violation of the dignity of the human person, we can assume that the eight dimensions of the nature of the human person examined in Chapter 3 could equally be applied to the phenomenon of sin. These eight dimensions must surely throw some light on the various ways it is possible for human beings to behave inhumanly towards each other or with regard to themselves. In fact, it would be possible to compose a very penetrating examination of conscience around these eight dimensions of what it means to be human — or inhuman. This examination of conscience would be based on how our current understanding of the dignity of the human person 'integrally and adequately considered' has broadened our sensitivity with regard to what should be considered to be 'sin" in this first sense. For instance, being more aware of the 'interdependence' dimension of being human will make us very sensitive to the dehumanizing effect that inhuman social structures can have on human persons and on life in general. John Paul II has emphasized this in his 1991 encyclical letter *Centesimus Annus*:

> The decisions which create a human environment can give rise to specific structures of sin which impede the full realization of those who are in any way oppressed by them. To destroy such structures and replace them with more authentic forms of living in community is a task which demands courage and patience. (n. 38)

This examination of conscience would also have to take account of how the voices of women theologians are sharpening our sensitivity. For instance, it would even have to pay attention to what Valerie Saiving would term 'specifically feminine sins' ('The human situation: a feminine view' in Carol P. Christ and Judith Paskow (eds), *Womanspirit Rising: A Feminist Reader in Religion* (Harper Forum, 1979), p. 37). She is very conscious that a woman who is a mother and who 'knows the profound experience of self-transcending love' might be tempted to try to sustain a 'perpetual I–Thou relationship'. That would be 'deadly', remarks Saiving. She goes on to explain why: 'A woman can give too much of herself, so that nothing remains of her own uniqueness; she can become merely an emptiness, almost a zero, without value to herself, to her fellow men (*sic!*), or, perhaps, even to God'. This leads her to note that 'pride' and 'will-to-power' are not typically feminine

forms of sin. The list she offers for a feminine examination of conscience is:

> ... triviality, distractibility, and diffuseness; lack of an organizing
> center or focus; dependence on others for one's own self-definition;
> tolerance at the expense of standards of excellence; inability to respect
> the boundaries of privacy; sentimentality, gossipy sociability, and
> mistrust of reason — in short, underdevelopment or negation of the self.
> (ibid.)

Even if Saiving is accurate in her analysis, the above list should
offer no comfort to men. Patriarchy encourages and feeds off the
above characteristics. To the extent that women allow themselves
to remain underdeveloped in these ways, there is even less hope of
men being converted and freed from their own typically masculine
forms of sin. Men and women stand in interdependence on each
other for this mutual healing process.

As already mentioned, many moral theologians prefer to use the
terms 'wrong' or 'evil' rather than 'sin' meant in this first sense. Since
sin in its primary meaning is really a theological word referring to a
person's relationship to God, they suggest that it might be better to
avoid the word 'sin' when we are speaking of an action without any
reference to the person doing it. Nevertheless, in practice it is
impossible to have a human action without a human agent. Moreover, as we have seen in the previous chapter, the agent's interpretation of what he or she is doing has to be considered in determining
the 'objective' nature of the action. Despite all that, it can be helpful
to be more careful about how we use the word 'sin'.

The second and fundamental meaning of sin refers directly to my
relationship as a unique human person to God. Clearly, this second
meaning of sin cannot properly be understood in isolation from the
first meaning we have been considering. Sin in this second sense
involves the exercise of my inner freedom in such a way that I reject
the offer of life and love that God is making to me. Two points are
of major importance here. One is that sin in this sense is going
against the grain. It is going against a deep inclination within us
towards our true good and happiness. That is why sin in this sense is
often spoken of in terms of alienation. It is being untrue to our real
selves. The other point of major importance is that God's offer of
life and love only comes to me through my life as a person in this
world. In other words, the eight dimensions of what is involved in
the dignity of a human person are in fact the medium through which

I encounter God's call to me in this life. That is why this second and fundamental meaning of sin cannot properly be understood in isolation from the first meaning we looked at.

This links in with one of the fundamental truths on which this book is based, namely, that our response to God lies in the way we live out our lives rather than in the verbal professions of faith we articulate. Who we are, the beliefs we genuinely own, are revealed in the way we knowingly live our lives. That is why I have insisted that the theme of evangelization cannot be divorced from that of morality. To reduce faith to something purely internal is to fall back into some kind of dualism. I do not respond to God's invitation by some kind of disembodied, internal word of acceptance or refusal. God's invitation to me is myself, the person I am, considered in all the different dimensions of human personhood examined in Chapter 3. Whether my response to this invitation is one of acceptance or rejection will take shape and be revealed in my life. The way I live my life constitutes my faith-response to God. That is true of every person who has ever lived, whether they be Christian or not. This is not to deny, of course, that the Christian faith, as we saw in the previous chapter, is a unique gift which naturally colours the way a Christian responds to God in his or her life.

When we use sin in this second sense, we tend to make a distinction between 'sin' in the singular and 'sins' in the plural. 'Sin' in the singular refers to my basic disposition *vis-à-vis* God. That basic disposition is essentially personal. It only takes shape in me as a person as I respond to life as it comes to me in the various dimensions of my personhood. In other words, it is in the decisions of my life that I come to shape the person I choose to be. This is a gradual, fluctuating process, frequently involving considerable ambiguity.

It is important, therefore, to recognize the limited character of our human freedom. The person I become is a complex mixture of the person I have chosen to be and the person which other people, events and external factors have fashioned me to be. I used the phrase 'victim of sin' earlier. All of us, to a lesser or greater extent, are 'victims of sin' — just as, conversely, all of us are 'inheritors of grace'. These two phrases refer to the negative and positive sides of my personality which I have acquired as a result of my upbringing and the relationships and events of my early life. Much of this process may well have been outside my control. I may have had little choice in it. These aspects of my personality are now a part of me. I cannot rid myself of them simply by disowning them. However, they do not yet constitute the 'real' me.

The 'real' me takes shape in the mysterious inner core of my being and is fashioned precisely by my gradually identifying myself with the 'victim of sin' or the 'inheritor of grace' side of my given personality. Naturally I have to 'own' both these sides of myself but I do not have to 'identify' myself with both of them. The exercise of my basic freedom gradually takes shape as I come to direct my life in one or other of these two directions. This will take time as I progressively commit myself more and more to either the human or inhuman side of the personality which I have received.

In the case of my settling for the 'sin' option, therefore, this basic disposition gradually becomes fashioned in me as, by freely giving in to the inhuman tendencies I find in myself, I identify myself with this side of me. This gradually becomes the 'real me'. Nevertheless, this 'fundamental option', as it is sometimes called, is not some kind of internal choice I arrive at without any connection with life as it goes on around me. It is actually the end result of a process involving the dehumanizing actions I commit myself to as I live out my everyday life. It is when we want to refer to these dehumanizing actions that we are inclined to speak of 'sins' in the plural.

Although this fundamental option is never completely definitive in this life (Rahner stresses the hopeful side of this truth), it can become sufficiently definitive to constitute my basic stance as a person. This may be the result of a life lived in a generally dehumanizing direction through a whole accumulation of decisions, none of them of major importance in themselves; or it may come to a head in some decision which violates human dignity in some matter of major importance. Obviously this second scenario could scarcely happen out of the blue.

Throughout life our relationship with God is lived through the medium of our relationships with our fellow human beings and the rest of creation. This is where we make our real confession of faith — in action. This is also where our rejection of God takes place. Sin should not be envisaged as some kind of direct refusal of God's love. When we sin, we do not turn towards God and reject him face to face. Offending God is not the purpose we have in mind when we sin. To sin does not mean that we intend evil *precisely as evil*. Human beings cannot operate in that way. What happens is that we knowingly allow ourselves to be enticed by some lesser good which is out of proportion to the harm done to others (or ourselves) by our action. Our decision is disordered. We are choosing what we see is good 'for us' here and now. But because of the harm it will do to other human persons, or even to ourselves in the longer term, it is a disordered choice of some good. In other words, seen against this broader backcloth what we are choosing is not really good at all. It is a refusal to transcend ourselves. As such, it does not really fit in with our basic criterion of the good of the human person 'integrally and adequately considered'. Such a decision, therefore, is not truly human. It is neither wise nor loving.

Sin consists in my knowingly and deliberately choosing to act in such an inhuman way to the detriment of myself or my fellow human beings. That is what offends God. Aquinas pointed this out centuries ago. My own rough paraphrase of *Contra Gentiles*, III, n. 122 is: 'God is not offended by us except insofar as we harm ourselves and/or each other'. It is through such inhuman behaviour that sin stamps its image on my person. I fashion myself into a sinner through sinning. When such behaviour seriously violates my own human dignity or that of others, my relationship with God is seriously affected. Although sin in this sense implies culpability, nevertheless there is far more to sin than is conveyed by the term 'culpability'. By the same token, there is also far more to sin than bad intention.

John Finnis, in his book *Fundamentals of Ethics* (Oxford University Press, 1983), expresses very clearly the point I have been making:

> Whenever we choose anything, we choose it because it seems to offer some good, some intelligible advantage or opportunity. But what intelligible advantage could anyone see in being selfish rather than loving, or unreasonable rather than reasonable, *apart from the advantages offered by some particular objective, or some particular option for action by him?*
>
> No. One chooses to be selfish and unreasonable in the free choices one makes to do a selfish and unreasonable act . . . (p. 143)

Finnis quotes the example of the four Athenians who, unlike Socrates, chose to accept the commission to liquidate Leon of Salamis. He imagines how they must have rationalized their choice *en route*. They would be trying to persuade themselves that they had good solid reasons for their choice and 'were not making themselves selfish, unjust, unreasonable or immoral'. Nevertheless,

Finnis concludes, 'unless and until they repudiated their act as not merely regrettable and "tragic" but actually wrongful (their own wrong), they were what they had made themselves by their free choice: unjust, murderous . . .' (ibid.).

A more contemporary application of this understanding of how we become sinners through our sinful choices is given by Anthony Kenny in his book *The Logic of Deterrence* (Firethorn Press, 1985). Although his argument against nuclear deterrence has been challenged, his description of how a major sinful choice makes a person a sinner loses none of its power. He is envisaging a scenario where deterrence has broken down and a person is faced with 'a choice of carrying out the deterrent threat, or of forfeiting the good things which the deterrent was meant to protect':

> If my [pro-deterrent] friend says that if, God forbid, it ever did come to such a point, then obviously the only thing to do is to surrender — if he says that, then I know that fundamentally we are morally at one, and we can settle down in a comparatively relaxed way to discuss questions of risk and expense. But if he says 'Well, I hate to have to say it, but if you are committed to the deterrent, you have to stick to what you believe in and must go right on and use it if it ever comes to the crunch' — if he says that and means it, then I can only tell him, quite soberly, that he is a man with murder in his heart. (p. 56)

Conversion

What Finnis does not mention here is how this repudiation comes about. This is the heart of the mystery of conversion. Christian faith insists that this process of conversion is impossible without the grace of God. However, that does not imply that it is a process which is completely beyond human analysis and understanding. The human processes through which life-giving healing takes place are the medium through which God's grace works its down-to-earth miracles.

As we have seen earlier in this chapter, experience suggests that in some mysterious way the deeply traumatic 'rock bottom' event of human failure, whether personal or communal, often seems to be the birth-pangs accompanying the birth of the conversion process. The new life which emerges needs to grow and develop. This is a process which takes place over time. Like any growth process, *en route* it needs to work through various stages, some of them marked by other major or minor versions of the 'death–resurrection' experience.

The expression 'commit sin' is significant. It suggests that in sinning we *commit ourselves*. In the conversion process, as Finnis rightly insists, we need to repudiate that commitment of ourselves. However, the deeper the various dimensions of our being have been committed in our sin, the lengthier is likely to be the gradual process of repudiation.

Here, too, Gabriel Daly's quasi-evolutionary approach to sin can help us. There is a danger of looking on conversion as a return to where we were initially — as though we had somehow fallen below our usual level of perfection! Daly reminds us that we are on a journey towards being 'fully human'. An *en route* experience of failure and redemption, sin and conversion, is bound to be a trans-formative experience. It is neither a 'return to go' as in a Monopoly game nor a going back to the point where we left the path. Because it is person-transforming as an experience, we ourselves will be different because of it — wiser, no doubt, and probably more understanding and compassionate. In a sense the journey itself will be different because of this transformation of the traveller. After all, the journey is really a pilgrimage and the purpose of a pilgrimage is the deepening conversion of the pilgrims just as much as their arrival at a particular destination.

Dorothee Sölle has written very movingly about her pilgrim journey through the devastating experience of the breakdown of her marriage. When she was at rock bottom she found strength in the words Paul heard in his hour of weakness: 'My grace is enough for you: my power is at its best in weakness' (2 Cor 12:9). This led Paul himself to comment: 'For it is when I am weak that I am strong' (v. 10). Dorothee Sölle describes her own personal experience of this dying and rising process:

> I began to an infinitesimal degree to accept that my husband was going another way, his own way. I had come to the end and God had torn up the first plan. He did not comfort me like a psychologist, who would have explained to me that this was foreseeable. He did not offer me the usual social consolations; he threw me face down on the floor. It was not death that I wanted for myself, nor was it life either. It was another death. Later I noticed that all those who believe limp a little, like Jacob after he had struggled with the angel. They have already died once. One cannot wish this on anyone, but one cannot attempt to spare them the lesson either. There is as little substitute for the experience of faith as

there is for the experience of love. (Quoted in Dietmar Mieth, 'The ethic of failure and beginning again: a forgotten perspective in theological ethics', *Concilium* (1990/5), p. 48)

Perhaps Sölle is reminding us that forgiveness and the human process through which it is experienced is an essential dimension of what it means to be human. According to Daly the human pilgrimage would proceed from the sub-humanity of sin, via the humanity of forgiveness, towards the fullness of humanity. This fullness will only be found in the kingdom, even though we are trying to sow its seeds in the midst of all the ambiguities of life today.

Epilogue

DIALOGUE, DIVERSITY AND TRUTH:
THE VOCATION OF THE MORAL THEOLOGIAN
IN THE ROMAN CATHOLIC CHURCH TODAY

It is not easy being a moral theologian today. The new questions being raised by modern advances in science and technology are exceedingly complicated. Moreover, of their very nature moral questions are not just theoretical issues. Important and urgent decisions have to be faced on issues which are matters of public debate. Added to this, the moral theologian cannot ignore contemporary discussions about the nature of human knowledge and the role of experience, which necessarily is historical and cultural, in the development of our knowledge. The moral theologian today is under pressure to take part in a whole variety of different dialogues if he or she is to make a contribution towards the common search to discover how our human family can be as human as possible in our world today.

In 1990 the Congregation for the Doctrine of the Faith (CDF) issued an Instruction entitled *The Ecclesial Vocation of the Theologian.* This Instruction is intended to assist theologians in their vocation. I would like to dialogue with this Instruction specifically as a moral theologian. In the course of this dialogue I hope I will be open to being challenged by it. I hope, too, that the reader will allow me to put questions to it, when this is appropriate. Such dialogue is both possible and beneficial since, as fellow Christians, its authors and I share a common commitment to striving for what is most truly human in the light of our common faith in the Gospel and the Church. Such an 'in-house' exercise of dialogue in the search for truth is perhaps a fitting way to conclude this book. My dialogue with the Instruction will be under nine headings.

1 The vocation of the moral theologian

Among the vocations awakened . . . by the Spirit in the church is that of the theologian. His role is to pursue in a particular way an ever deeper understanding of the word of God found in the inspired Scriptures and handed on by the living tradition of the church. He does this in communion with the magisterium, which has been charged with the responsibility of preserving the deposit of faith. (n. 6)

The title of the Instruction coins the phrase, 'ecclesial vocation of the theologian'. This is a very helpful and positive notion. Naturally, I would not understand that as implying that the vocation of the moral theologian is confined to his or her role within the Church and still less to his or her relationship with the papal and episcopal teaching authority in the Church. Throughout this book I have been stressing that moral theology involves listening to and dialoguing with Christians of other Churches as well as with men and women of other faiths and none. This dialogue has a genuine learning intent: it is not just an evangelistic ploy. As n. 10 of the Instruction acknowledges, moral theology also involves dialogue with the human sciences and with philosophical thought. All these dimensions of dialogue pertain to the vocation of the moral theologian. It is a dialogue which is more likely to take place in the setting of the university (and not just the Catholic or Christian university) or even through the medium of debate in the mass media. Understanding the expression 'ecclesial vocation' as embracing these dimensions, I am sure moral theologians will be grateful to the Instruction for giving such a positive recognition of their role.

The Instruction is stressing something very important when it refers to the vocation of the moral theologian as 'ecclesial'. Bishop James Malone, a former president of the US National Conference of Catholic Bishops, has reminded us that 'Theologians . . . are not self-employed: they live in the ecclesial community and their work is a public function for the community. A church devoid of theologians or a church which fails to respect the theological enterprise forfeits its sense of identity and its potential for witness in the wider society' ('How bishops and theologians relate', *Origins* (31 July 1986), pp. 169–74 at p. 172). Furthermore, this is not a matter of one-way traffic. The Church might need moral theologians, but moral theologians need the Church too. Cardinal Ratzinger writes: 'A church without theology is impoverished and blind. A theology without a church, however, soon dissolves into arbitrary theory' ('The Church and the theologian', *Origins* (8 May 1986), pp. 761–70 at p. 763).

In various places the Instruction suggests that theology, and so presumably moral theology too, plays an important and necessary role in the life of the Church. For instance, we read:

> *Benefiting from the work of theologians,* it [the Magisterium] refutes objections to and distortions of the faith and promotes, with the authority received from Jesus Christ, new and deeper comprehension, clarification, and application of revealed doctrine. (n. 21)
>
> Theology and the Magisterium are of diverse natures and missions and cannot be confused. Nonetheless they fulfil *two vital roles in the church which must interpenetrate and enrich each other for the service of the People of God.* (n. 40 — italics mine throughout)

What I would draw from these and other passages is that at least part of the vocation of the moral theologian is to be of service to all who are called to exercise the teaching vocation in the Church. The Instruction leaves us in no doubt that the CDF sees this teaching vocation to be one of crucial importance in the Church. It involves 'preserving, explaining and spreading' 'the truth of Christ which sets us free' (nn. 14, 3). To acknowledge the great importance of this teaching role would seem to imply that it should be approached with a particular sense of care and responsibility. Part of this care and responsibility involves using every means possible to ensure that the teacher is drawing on all the gifts of wisdom, insight and experience that the Spirit is making available to the Church in diverse ways.

This brings up the first question I would raise in my dialogue with the Instruction. Is it inclined to identify the actual function of teaching (magisterium) in the Church too much with the pope, assisted by the Roman Curia, and the bishops? As Nicholas Lash pointed out in the course of the 1989 meeting of the Catholic Theological Association of Great Britain, to do this would be to reduce the function of teaching, which is widespread and multi-faceted throughout the Church, to the activity of only some of its functionaries, important though they may be. Based on his own original research an important study of the use of the term 'magisterium' was published some years ago by Yves Congar (*Revue des sciences philosophiques et théologiques* (1976), pp. 85–112 — English translation in Charles Curran and Richard A. McCormick (eds), *Readings in Moral Theology* No. 3 (Mahwah, NJ; Paulist Press, 1982), pp. 297–331). This revealed that restricting the term 'magisterium', which literally means 'teaching function', to the teaching function of the pope, assisted by the Roman Curia, and the bishops is not in keeping with the traditional usage in the Church. Moreover, it tends to suggest that the pope, the Roman Curia and the bishops are the 'teachers' in the Church, while all other Christians have a different function which is not really part of the Church's teaching function (magisterium). In fact, John Paul II's great emphasis on the responsibility of all Christians for the work of evangelization is a recognition of the shared teaching vocation of all members of the Church, to be exercised in our different roles. Consequently, for the rest of this chapter. I will use the expression 'papal and episcopal magisterium' whenever I am referring to that special part of the Church's teaching function which is carried out by the pope, assisted by the Roman Curia, and the bishops.

2 Listening to experience and the human sciences

The Instruction (n. 8) states that 'the object of theology is the Truth which is the living God and His plan for salvation revealed in Jesus Christ'. It goes on to explain the task of theology as follows:

> Theology's proper task is to understand the meaning of revelation and this, therefore, requires the utilization of philosophical concepts which provide 'a solid and correct understanding of man, the world, and God' and can be employed in a reflection upon revealed doctrine. The historical disciplines are likewise necessary for the theologian's investigations. This is due chiefly to the historical character of revelation itself which has been communicated to us in 'salvation history'. Finally, a consultation of the 'human sciences' is also necessary to understand better the revealed truth about man and the moral norms for his conduct, setting these in relation to the sound findings of such sciences. (n. 10)

Leaving aside its sexist language, as a moral theologian I find this a very affirming passage. What the Instruction calls 'the truth of Christ which sets us free' is the ultimate foundation of our belief that morality matters — to God and to us. That is why the Instruction rightly stresses the importance of a 'solid and correct understanding' of ourselves as human beings, of our world and of God. To achieve this the Instruction recognizes that the human sciences have an indispensable role to play. They help us to delve more deeply into the truth about ourselves as bodily, sexual, interdependent, social, cultural and historical human beings. In this way the revealed truth that morality matters in our covenant relationship with God is opened up more clearly to our minds as we come to grasp what is entailed in wise and loving living as human beings.

3   Collaborative relations between the papal and episcopal magisterium and moral theologians

This important issue is dealt with in section IV.A of the Instruction. Earlier in the Instruction (section I) we are given a very positive exposition of the vocation of the theologian. I am sure that most theologians will find that a very helpful and affirmative section. The excellence of that treatment might explain my disappointment at this section on collaboration. I would have liked the Instruction to have offered some positive suggestions as to how precisely these 'two vital roles in the church' (theology and the papal and episcopal magisterium) can best work in collaboration with each other so that they can 'interpenetrate and enrich each other for the service of the People of God' (n. 40). Instead of focusing on such mutual inter-penetration and enrichment, this section concentrates mainly on insisting on the theologian's duty to accept and proclaim the teaching of the papal and episcopal magisterium. This is highlighted in n. 22:

> Collaboration between the theologian and the magisterium occurs in a special way when the theologian receives the canonical mission or the mandate to teach. In a certain sense, such collaboration becomes a participation in the work of the magisterium, linked as it then is by a juridic bond. The theologian's code of conduct, which obviously has its origin in the service of the word of God, is here reinforced by the commitment the theologian assumes in accepting his office, making the profession of faith and taking the oath of fidelity.
>
> From this moment on, the theologian is officially charged with the task of presenting and illustrating the doctrine of the faith in its integrity and with full accuracy. (n. 22)

In dialoguing with this Instruction, Francis Sullivan ('The theologian's ecclesial vocation and the 1990 CDF Instruction', *Theological Studies* (1991), pp. 51–68), suggests that this is 'taking a one-sidedly juridical approach to the question of the collaboration between theologians and the magisterium' (p. 59). For him 'the danger in the juridical approach of this Instruction is that it suggests that ultimately there is only one kind of teaching authority in the church, the hierarchical, and that all teaching authority must necessarily be a participation in this' (p. 60).

The irony is that, despite its recommendation of dialogue between the papal and episcopal magisterium and theologians, the Instruction itself seems to have overlooked a golden opportunity for such dialogue in its own composition. In 1975 the International Theological Commission published a document entitled *Theses on the Relationship between the Ecclesiastical Magisterium and Theology*. This document came from a body which, at the time, enjoyed the respect of a wide spectrum of theologians and also had the confidence of the CDF itself and met under its general auspices. The theses it put forward offered very constructive proposals for collaboration and were welcomed by most theologians. Like Sullivan I find it hard to understand why the present Instruction, at least judging by its content and references, does not seem to have made 'significant use' of this document of the International Theological Commission. There is a note of sadness in Sullivan's comment that 'there is little or no evidence of such a dialogue in the present Instruction' (p. 52). Incidentally, drawing on the International Theological Commission document I offer some suggestions on the conduct of this important dialogue in my essay 'The role of the moral theologian in the life of the Church' (in Raphael Gallagher and Brendan McConvery (eds), *History and Conscience* (Gill and Macmillan, 1989), pp. 8–23; a revised version of a paper originally presented at a collaborative seminar between members of the Episcopal Conference of England and Wales and a group of British moral theologians).

4 *The authority of moral teaching*

Jesus Christ promised the assistance of the Holy Spirit to the church's pastors so that they could fulfill their assigned task of teaching the Gospel and authentically interpreting revelation. In particular he bestowed on them the charism of infallibility in matters of faith and morals. . . . (n. 15).

What concerns morality can also be the object of the authentic Magisterium because the Gospel, being the Word of Life, inspires and guides the whole sphere of human behaviour. The Magisterium, therefore, has the task of discerning, by means of judgements normative for the consciences of believers, those acts which in themselves conform to the demands of faith and foster their expression in life and those which, on the contrary, because intrinsically evil, are incompatible with such demands. By reason of the connection between the orders of creation and redemption and by reason of the necessity, in view of salvation, of knowing and observing the whole moral law, the competence of the Magisterium also extends to that which concerns the natural law.

Revelation also contains moral teachings which *per se* could be known

3

by natural reason. Access to them, however, is made difficult by man's
sinful condition. It is a doctrine of faith that these moral norms can be
infallibly taught by the magisterium. (n. 16)

Even infallible teaching retains its historical, and so non-final,
character. This point is well put by Avery Dulles when he insists that
'even dogmatic declarations cannot be final'. He goes on to quote
from the International Theological Commission's 1990 paper on the
interpretation of dogma: 'The definition of a dogma, therefore, is
never just the end of a development, but always a new beginning'.
Dulles reminds us that 'even after the magisterium has spoken,
theologians play an important role in the reception and interpretation of doctrinal declarations' ('The magisterium, theology and
dissent', *Origins* (28 March 1991), pp. 692–6 at p. 693). Richard
McCormick makes a similar point when he states that 'honest theological input is called for both before *and after* official statements'
(*The Christian Century* (8–15 August 1990), p. 735). This would
obviously also apply to such a basic moral truth as the revealed
teaching that our moral life is relevant to our covenant relationship
with God. Obviously, what that revealed truth implies in terms of
the kind of moral life demanded of men and women today pertains
to the common search in which we are engaged to find out how we
can best live wise and loving lives at this stage in human history.

The charism of infallibility does not promise the Church any
short-cut to arriving at the kind of truth we are searching for in
moral theology when we are trying to deepen our understanding of
ourselves as bodily, sexual, interdependent, social, cultural and
historical human beings. It is true we can trust that divine assistance
will be with us in this search; but that trust is only justified if we
are prepared to take the necessary steps to achieve the knowledge
and understanding we are looking for. As the Instruction notes in
n. 10, one of these 'necessary' steps is a 'consultation of the human
sciences'. In other words, divine assistance in attaining the truth
learned through experience involves listening to relevant experience
wherever it is to be found.

I find n. 16 of the Instruction very supportive of the basic theme of
this book in that it insists that no dimension of human life is outside
the concern of the Gospel. In other words, the whole of human life is
the concern of the Church. The Church refuses to withdraw into the
sacristy as some people, especially some politicians, would like it to.
I would not understand that passage as claiming that the Church has

specialist knowledge of its own which makes it uniquely competent to pass a definitive judgement on any or every moral issue under the sun. 'Competence' in this connection carries more the meaning of 'legitimate concern' rather than 'knowledge sufficient to pass a correct judgement'. When it has that too, as it would when the relevant knowledge is available and it has done its homework properly, its judgement could indeed be said to be 'normative for the consciences of believers'. The relationship between conscience and particular moral rules as taught by the Church has already been discussed in Chapter 4. It should go without saying, of course, that the Church's claim to be competent to teach on moral issues in no way implies any claim to competence to teach infallibly on all such issues.

The final paragraph of n. 16 quoted above is interpreted by Sullivan in an exclusive sense. In other words, no naturally known moral truths can be infallibly taught other than those contained in revelation: 'The only naturally knowable moral norms which this document says can be infallibly taught are those which are also contained in revelation' (p. 57).

5 Divine assistance

The Instruction repeatedly claims 'divine assistance' for the work of the papal and episcopal magisterium. No Catholic would want to deny that. However, this divine assistance should not be understood in a fundamentalist sense as some kind of directly revealed new and exclusive knowledge given to the pope and the bishops or the CDF and its select consultors. This 'divine assistance' is also at work in the rich variety of gifts found throughout the whole Church — and beyond. One of these gifts is that of theology, including moral theology. And, as we have seen, moral theology has to listen to the voice of the Spirit even in 'foreign prophecy' beyond the confines of. the Church.

Everyone except the die-hard reactionaries in the Church would accept that divine assistance was given in abundance to the Second Vatican Council. Yet it would be absurd to suggest that that divine assistance was limited to the activity of the bishops in their formal voting sessions. Divine assistance was surely at work in the collaborative work of theologians and bishops as they struggled to express in the draft documents the richest insights of the Church and human wisdom at that time. Divine assistance was certainly at work in the tension-filled process which led to the rejection of the schemata prepared for the Council by the pre-conciliar Preparatory Commissions. This freed the bishops to work collaboratively with the Church's best theologians. Remembering Simmel's wise words, quoted in Chapter 3, about the indispensable role of conflict in human social and group processes (cf. p. 46 above), we can assume too that divine assistance was operative within (and not just despite) the many conflicts and intrigues that occurred throughout the four sessions of Vatican II.

This leads me to raise another question in my dialogue with the Instruction. Does it not tend to give the impression that the 'divine assistance' enjoyed by the papal and episcopal magisterium operates independently of its collaboration with others in the Church through whom God's Spirit is working? I would suggest that the warning voiced in n. 40, 'To succumb to the temptation of dissent is to allow the "leaven of infidelity to the Holy Spirit" to start to work', needs to be balanced by recognizing a similar temptation for those called to the vocation of papal and episcopal magisterium in the Church. That would be the temptation to believe that they can lay an exclusive claim to divine assistance or to forget that divine assistance operates through the variety of gifts found in the Church and beyond. Karl Rahner issued a warning in 1964 which still has a message for us today:

> It [executive authority in the church] must keep alive the consciousness that it is a duty and not a gracious condescension when it accepts suggestions from 'below'; that it must not from the start pull all the strings; and that the higher and, in fact, charismatic wisdom can sometimes be with the subordinate, and that the charismatic wisdom of office may consist in not shutting itself off from such higher wisdom. (*The Dynamic Element in the Church* (Burns & Oates, 1964), p. 71)

Round about the same time, Brian Wicker was suggesting that the teaching authority exercised by the seminar leader provides an alternative model for teaching authority in the Church (*Culture and Theology* (Sheed & Ward, 1966), pp. 274–8). Whereas the lecturer tends to be seen as the teacher in whom all knowledge resides, the role of the seminar leader is more that of an enabler in the learning process. The seminar leader ensures that all the relevant wisdom in the group is made available to the whole seminar class. On top of this the seminar leader makes sure adequate background reading is done and also contributes his or her specialist knowledge of the subject. In this way, he or she makes sure that the whole seminar takes note of relevant knowledge, past and present, which is to be found beyond the group's own resources. In line with that model I believe that one of the most inspired and major exercises of papal magisterium in recent centuries has been the calling of the Second Vatican Council by Pope John XXIII.

There is no doubt that belief in the Holy Spirit active within the Church — and beyond — is part of the core of our Christian world-view. Nevertheless, to appeal to the guidance of the Holy Spirit does not provide an escape clause freeing us from the discipline of competent moral enquiry and analysis. A warning given by Gerard Hughes on this point is very timely and wise:

> In practice the appeal to tradition and to teaching authority tends to short-circuit the need for proper inquiry and for argument which will withstand criticism in open debate. These are the normal human means to the attainment of truth, which we ignore at our peril. To this, of course it might be replied that it is precisely the function of the Spirit in guiding the church to enable us to avoid the errors to which even the best-conducted human inquiry is . . . all too liable. The question then is, what requirements on our human cooperation are there if we are to have any well-founded confidence in the guidance of the Spirit? I suspect that the ultimate cause of disagreement in moral theology today stems from a notion of revelation and the guidance of the Spirit in the church which is largely independent of human cooperation, and a contrasting notion in which such guidance is to be expected only when we have in fact done what is humanly possible. I think one of the most valuable aspects of the natural law tradition in moral theology is that it comes down firmly in favour of this latter view . . .
>
> We cannot confidently lay claim to the guidance of the Spirit, whether as individuals or as a church, unless we take the normal human means to try to arrive at the truth. ('Natural law ethics and moral theology', *The Month* (1987), pp. 102–3)

In fact, it could be argued that, faced with an instance of an inadequate exercise of Church teaching, the action of the Spirit might well be found in those who help the Church recognize this inadequacy by solidly critical analysis and argumentation or by pointing out its lack of grounding in true human experience. Mahoney suggests that this cannot be ruled out as an interpretation of the negative reception given to *Humanae Vitae*: 'For the influence of the Holy Spirit in the hearts of the faithful, as described by Pope Paul, is envisaged purely as disposing them to be receptive, whereas it might be a more positive one of refining, qualifying, or even correcting the papal teaching' (*The Making of Moral Theology*, p. 295).

6 The essential distinction between disagreement and dissent

> The right conscience of the Catholic theologian presumes not only faith in the word of God, whose riches he must explore, but also love for the church, from whom he receives his mission, and respect for her divinely assisted magisterium. Setting up a supreme magisterium of conscience in opposition to the magisterium of the church means adopting a principle of free examination incompatible with the economy of revelation and its transmission in the church and thus also with a correct understanding of theology and the role of the theologian. (n. 38)

I have always been unhappy with the term 'dissent'. It is a negative word. It carries the same overtones as terms like deny, oppose, contradict. There is nothing positive or affirmative about it. In fact, that is why much of what the Instruction says about dissent is very helpful. As Sullivan has pointed out, the Instruction goes out of its way to pin-point the kind of position it is referring to when it uses the term 'dissent'. What it means by dissent is spelt out in n. 32:

> The magisterium has drawn attention several times to the serious harm done to the community of the church by *attitudes of general opposition to church teaching which even come to expression in organized groups.* In his apostolic exhortation *Paterna cum Benevolentia,* Paul VI offered a diagnosis of this problem, which is still apropos. In particular, he addresses here that *public opposition to the magisterium of the church also called dissent,* which must be distinguished from the situation of personal difficulties treated above. (n. 32 — italics mine)

It seems clear, too, that the attitude the Instruction describes by 'dissent' involves advocating a kind of private judgement. For instance, n. 32 speaks of 'the tendency to regard a judgement as having all the more validity to the extent that it proceeds from the individual relying upon his own powers' and so 'freedom of thought comes to oppose the authority of tradition which is considered a cause of servitude'. The attitude the Instruction condemns as 'dissent' believes that 'a teaching handed on and generally received is *a priori* suspect and its truth contested' and that 'freedom of judgement . . . is more important than the truth itself'. Later the Instruction describes dissent as an attitude which claims 'a kind of "parallel magisterium" of theologians' (n. 34) and that they are 'setting up a supreme magisterium of conscience in opposition to the magisterium of the church' (n. 38).

In n. 33 the Instruction clarifies still further what it means by 'dissent':

> In its most radical form [dissent] aims at *changing the church following a model of protest which takes its inspiration from political society.* More frequently, it is asserted that *the theologian is not bound to adhere to any magisterial teaching unless it is infallible* . . . Doctrines proposed without exercise of the charism of infallibility are said to have *no obligatory character about them, leaving the individual completely at liberty to adhere to them or not.* The theologian would accordingly be totally free to raise doubts or reject the noninfallible teaching of the magisterium, particularly in the case of specific moral norms. (n. 33 — italics mine)

Hence, the kind of 'dissent' that the Instruction is rejecting is a dissent which would claim to be a kind of 'parallel magisterium' working 'in opposition to and in competition with the authentic magisterium' (n. 34) and emanating from an attitude of 'general opposition to church teaching' (n. 32).

It seems clear that what the Instruction means by 'dissent' is very different from the problem that arises when a theologian finds he or she is unable to accept a particular piece of authentic teaching coming within the category of teaching which the Instruction terms 'non-irreformable' (n. 28). After serious reflection such a theologian might consider that disagreement with this item of teaching is the only appropriate response he or she can give to this teaching. From his study of the Instruction Sullivan concludes that such disagreement is actually accepted by the document:

> In my judgment, it is certain that this Instruction does not rule out the possibility of legitimate interior non-assent to specific teachings of the ordinary, non-definitive magisterium. Rather, it seems to me clearly to recognize the compatibility of an attitude of *obsequium religiosum* with such well-founded nonassent. (p. 64)

It would seem, therefore, that the kind of thinking expressed by Ladislas Örsy in an earlier issue of *Theological Studies* is quite compatible with the theological position found in the Instruction:

> There is much among non-infallible teachings that is human opinion. It follows that the division of our beliefs into two neat categories, infallible and fallible, coupled with the suggestion that dissent from noninfallibly stated doctrine should be always permissible, is a simplistic approach to

a complex issue. Some of the non-infallibly stated doctrines may well be·
integral parts of the deposit of revelation. It follows also, with no less
force, that a good portion of the non-infallible propositions is no more
than respectable school opinion, and as such not part of the universally
held Catholic doctrine. ('Magisterium: assent and dissent', *Theological
Studies* (1987), pp. 485–6)

According to this approach, therefore, it is possible that disagreement might be an appropriate response in the case of some particular
instances of teaching authority in the area of non-infallible teaching.
Naturally, this could occur in some instances of teaching on specific
moral issues since often the truth of such teaching depends on the
adequacy of both the empirical evidence available and the philosophical analysis which is being used.

I know many moral theologians who disagree with certain points
of what the Instruction calls 'non-irreformable magisterial teaching'
(n. 28). However, I know of no moral theologian who dissents precisely in the technical sense meant by the CDF. In fact, with due
respect to the CDF I do not believe that even Charles Curran, despite
his own use of the term 'dissent', qualifies as a 'dissenter' in the strict
sense of the term. I feel sure that he does not hold the views ascribed
to 'dissenters' by the Instruction. For instance, he is certainly not an
advocate of a private judgement approach to moral issues. He does
not believe that 'a teaching handed on and generally received is *a
priori* suspect and its truth contested' and that 'freedom of judgement . . . is more important than the truth itself'. Neither would he
want to claim to be 'setting up a supreme magisterium of conscience
in opposition to the magisterium of the church' (n. 38). Nor is his
attitude one of 'general opposition to church teaching'. Lest this be
interpreted as special pleading by a colleague and friend, it might be
appropriate to quote from what Curran's own Ordinary, Bishop
Matthew Clark of Rochester, NY, wrote publicly about him on
12 March 1986 when he was under investigation by the CDF:

> As a theologian, Father Curran enjoys considerable respect not only in
> our diocese but across this country. He is unfailingly thorough and
> respectful in his exposition of the teaching of the church. Indeed, I have
> heard it said that few theologians have a better grasp of or express more
> clearly the fullness of the Catholic moral tradition. In instances when
> Father Curran offers theological views which appear to be at variance
> with the current official statements of the church, he always does so in a
> responsible manner. He is respectful of authority in the church, treating
> and referring to persons in authority in a most Christian manner.

Some members of the Catholic Church have occasionally depicted Father Curran as irreverent, disrespectful, disloyal and unprofessional. I believe that he is none of these. Such judgments of this good priest are sometimes written by those in the church who do not understand the probing and testing nature of the theological enterprise. This will remain a problem in our age of instant communication wherein theologians have no quiet corner in which to attempt to deepen their understanding of our faith. Our concern for this persistent difficulty should not grow out of proportion, allowing fear of confusion to end the necessary growth of theology . . .

Alteration of Father Curran's mandate to teach as a Roman Catholic theologian would be an extremely painful experience for all of us and doubly so because the pain would be born of a common and intense love for the church and a desire to be fully loyal to the Holy See. (*Origins* (13 April 1986), p. 694)

The Instruction's restriction of the meaning of 'dissent' is much to be welcomed. It provides moral theologians with a clear distinction between unacceptable dissent and the kind of disagreement which many moral theologians can recognize in themselves and which they believe comes from a very positive attitude towards teaching authority in the Church. It includes such positive elements as respect for tradition, concern for the truth, love of the Church, shared responsibility for the Church's mission in the world, commitment to Vatican II's call to dialogue in a common search for the truth, respect for the place of human reason in discovering and articulating our deepening understanding of the truth, responsibility towards those who are looking for help in major decisions affecting their personal or professional lives, etc. The term 'dissent' misses all this, as Örsy observes: 'The voice of a theologian proposing an answer different from the one given by those in authority may not be an act of dissent at all; rather, it may be a needed contribution to the development of doctrine, coming from someone who is assenting to every part of the revealed truth' ('Magisterium', p. 492). Moreover, the Instruction's restricted and more precise interpretation of 'dissent' should ease the minds of those who might be worried as to whether they could in conscience take the oath of fidelity in its current form. The *obsequium religiosum* pledged in the oath is not incompatible with actual disagreement with a particular instance of non-irreformable church teaching.

The Instruction (nn. 32–41) fears that those who come under its description of 'dissent' are really lacking in a deep faith in the

Church. To balance the equation I would put another question to the Instruction. Should it perhaps be open to the possibility that those lacking deep faith in the Church might be found in church groupings who actually pride themselves on their loyalty to the Church? For instance, might not an unwillingness to entertain in oneself or others any kind of critical approach to the Bible or Church teaching be a significant indication of a lack of faith in the Church? Judging by the correspondence columns in some of our religious newspapers, I get the impression that some Catholics today are haunted by a feeling of fear, suspicion and insecurity. It is almost as though they are afraid to trust the movement of the Holy Spirit within the Church. They see no place for real dialogue within the Church, and especially with those outside the Church, since dia-·logue involves listening in order to deepen our understanding of the Good News (*Gaudium et Spes*, n. 58; cf. also n. 44) and for them that is unthinkable. It is too threatening since it suggests that the Church is also a learning community which has to be open to change. Their fear is not unlike that of some of the early Christians who felt very threatened and insecure at the prospect of non-Jews being admitted to baptism (cf. Acts 15:1–2 and Gal 2:11–14).

The Instruction offers no encouragement to such an attitude. In n. 25 it insists on the importance of dialogue and acknowledges that the tensions of disagreement can work as 'a dynamic factor' in the Church. That indicates a real belief and trust in the Church. That is quite different to the attitude of fear and suspicion I mentioned, even though its adherents often claim to be the sole upholders of loyalty to the Church. I honestly believe that what is sometimes called 'loyal disagreement' in the Church is often an expression of a deep faith and great love in and for the Church.

7 Hostile and contrary feelings and love-inspired anger

Even when collaboration takes place under the best conditions the possibility cannot be excluded that tensions may arise between the theologian and the magisterium. The meaning attributed to such tensions and the spirit with which they are faced are not matters of indifference. If tensions do not spring from hostile and contrary feelings, they can become a dynamic factor, a stimulus to both the magisterium and theologians to fulfil their respective roles while practising dialogue. (n. 25)

I would suggest that the phrase 'hostile and contrary feelings' in the above passage should not be interpreted as meaning that there is no place for anger in the expression of criticism within the Church. As we saw in Chapter 5, women theologians have made us more aware of the importance for theology of tuning into and interpreting our feelings. The feeling of anger can be an indication that someone or something we reverence and hold dear is being mistreated.

The love of God made visible in Christ Jesus showed itself in Jesus' anger at the abuse of true religion by the religious leaders of his day. I would detect a similar note of anger in some of Bernard Häring's published utterances which, to an undiscerning reader, might suggest 'hostile and contrary feelings' towards the pope and his Curia. To my mind there is no doubt that Häring's anger has its roots in his love for the Church to which he has dedicated his life so faithfully for so many years. He is angered by certain actions which he regards as unworthy of the Church he loves. Admittedly anger has to give way to calmer and more reasonable discussion and that is also seen in what Häring has written. Nevertheless, the feeling of anger in people of good will and deep wisdom is very important. It can be a crucial element in the 'dynamic factor' mentioned in the Instruction. If love is a gift of the Spirit, surely so too is love-inspired anger.

8 Untimely public teaching

> Even if the doctrine of the faith is not in question, the theologian will not present his own opinions or divergent hypotheses as though they were non-arguable conclusions. Respect for the truth as well as for the people of God requires this discretion (cf. Rom 14:1–15; 1 Cor 8; 10:23–33). For the same reasons, the theologian will refrain from giving untimely public expression to them. (n. 27)

> The preceding considerations have a particular application to the case of the theologian who might have serious difficulties, for reasons which appear to him well founded, in accepting a non-irreformable magisterial teaching. (n. 28)

The Instruction (n. 28) speaks of 'non-irreformable magisterial teaching' and the preceding section insists that if a theologian does not agree with such teaching he must not present his own views as 'non-arguable conclusions'. The strangeness of the expression 'non-infallible' has often been commented on. For some reason a double negative is used in place of the more simple expression 'fallible'. Perhaps some kind of justification could be offered for the term 'non-infallible' but there would seem to be less justification for the expression 'non-irreformable'. To say that a particular instance of teaching is non-irreformable is surely to say that, in principle at least, it is reformable. Dulles prefers the 'reformable' option, understanding it to mean 'non-definitive', even though he comments that it is 'not wholly felicitous'. Noting that 'a reformable statement may be certain and may contain abiding truth', he goes on to warn that it would be wrong to interpret non-irreformable as meaning 'should be reformed' (p. 696, n. 12)! Despite that, he recognizes that 'such statement could, in principle, be erroneous' (p. 694). Hence, I would conclude that in those instances where there are good grounds for arguing that an item of non-irreformable teaching needs reforming and even correcting, such teaching is evidently also 'arguable'.

The Instruction is right to object to any theologians who might be so foolish as to present their own divergent views as 'non-arguable'. However, in my dialogue with the Instruction I would like to voice a difficulty which Roman Catholic moral theologians have to cope with from time to time. This occurs when official Vatican documents do the very thing that the Instruction objects to. In other words, in some instances they present arguable teaching almost as if it were non-arguable. Such is the case, for instance, when an Instruction claims to offer definitive teaching on a topic which is still a matter of deep controversy among moral theologians, or even when the prevailing opinion amongst most moral theologians favours the opposite view.

The Instruction asks theologians not to give 'untimely public expression' to their arguable divergent opinions. Theologians wishing to dialogue with the Instruction would probably want to make a similar request themselves. If some item of teaching is arguable and is in fact a matter of considerable argument among responsible theologians, it would not be unreasonable for theologians to ask that the Vatican should be wary of giving 'untimely public expression' to what it would claim to be definitive teaching on this topic. In fact, n. 24 of the Instruction concedes that, when appropriate, a theologian may 'raise questions regarding the timeliness' of papal or episcopal teaching.

This kind of concern would seem to lie behind some of the five ground rules with which Dulles concludes his article. He comments on the Instruction's invitation to bishops 'to maintain and develop relations of trust with theologians in the fellowship of charity and in their acceptance that they share one spirit in their acceptance and service of the word' (n. 42). His ground rules suggest practical ways in which the pope (with the Roman Curia) and the bishops can play their part in building these relations of trust and avoiding 'any abuse of authority'. Among the ground rules he offers are:

1. The magisterium can avoid issuing too many statements, especially statements that appear to carry with them an obligation to assent. Until the 20th century . . . popes issued relatively few doctrinal decisions and then only at the end of a long process of theological discussion . . . Wherever diversity seems to be tolerable, theologians and others should be given freedom to use their own good judgment. Newman, and later Pope John XXIII, were fond of the ancient dictum: '*In necessariis unitas, in dubiis libertas, in omnibus caritas*'. (This dictum is also quoted in *Gaudium et Spes*, n. 92, where Vatican II is encouraging dialogue and urging reverence for 'lawful diversity' — my comment.)

3. The magisterium should be on guard against efforts of any given school or party to gain official endorsement for its own theological positions. Before issuing binding statements of doctrine, the pope and bishops would do well to consult with theologians of different schools . . .

4. The hierarchy, before it speaks, should anticipate objections and seek to obviate them. This goal can more easily be achieved if preliminary drafts are published and subjected to open criticism. (p. 696)

Dulles has his eye particularly on the doctrinal field in these suggestions, but they would seem to apply with at least equal validity to how the pope (with the Roman Curia) and the bishops exercise their teaching role with regard to moral issues.

9 Timely public expression of disagreement

As we have seen, n. 27 of the Instruction insists that a theologian who disagrees with papal or episcopal teaching, even if it is 'non-. irreformable', should refrain from 'untimely' public expression of his or her disagreement. Jack Mahoney comments that the use of the word 'untimely' here suggests that the CDF is acknowledging that some public expression of disagreement can be 'timely' (*The Month* (1990), p. 308). This raises an issue which greatly exercises moral theologians. It is the fact that many of the questions they have to face are matters of public debate. What does their 'ecclesial vocation' demand of them when they are given the opportunity of contributing to this public debate and yet they are faced with papal, curial or episcopal teaching which they would view as 'untimely' in the sense explained above? This is the final question I would like to raise in my dialogue with the Instruction.

In the press conference for the publication of the Instruction, Cardinal Ratzinger referred to the case of a theologian who disagrees with some official teaching and commented: 'We have not excluded all kinds of publication, nor have we closed him up in suffering. The Vatican insists, however, that theologians must choose the proper place to expound their ideas' (*Origins* (July 1990), p. 119). Sullivan discusses the issue of the theologian voicing his or her disagreement and agrees substantially with the following position put forward by Dulles:

> I would say that the CDF rules out strident public dissent and recourse to the media to foment opposition in the church, but that it acknowledges the value of discreet and constructive criticism of authoritative documents. The instruction does not seem to me to forbid the airing of such criticisms in scholarly journals, theological conferences, classroom situations and other appropriate forums. What the authorities do not forbid is, I take it, still permitted. ('The question of dissent', *The Tablet* (18 August 1990), pp. 1033–4 at p. 1033)

I agree with Dulles and Sullivan that moral theologians should not use the media to 'foment opposition in the church'. Neither should we indulge in 'strident public dissent', especially when dissent is understood in the sense used by the Instruction. However, that is not the only scenario for the participation of moral theologians in public debate on moral issues. To join in a public debate and in the course of that debate to have the honesty to admit to difficulties or even disagreement with some elements of reformable Church teaching relevant to the issue under debate is something completely different to fomenting opposition in the Church or expressing strident public dissent. The only other alternative would seem to be to stay out of the debate altogether and restrict themselves to their scholarly journals and theological conferences. However, many moral theologians would interpret that as failing to accept the responsibility of their ecclesial vocation. Although I respect Dulles and Sullivan very highly as theologians, I do not find their position in this instance particularly helpful for the difficult position moral theologians find themselves in with regard to public debate of important ethical issues in society today. Maybe their suggestion about restricting any expression of one's difficulties to scholarly journals and theological conferences is influenced by the fact that they are both systematic theologians and perhaps many of the controversial issues in that field, though fundamentally of great importance, are of less immediate practical relevance and urgency and hence less likely to be debated in the public forum.

In contrast to that, the enormous advances in human knowledge and scientific technology which have taken place in recent years raise ethical issues of great complexity and vital importance. It is a sign of a healthy and mature society that these ethical issues are debated in the public arena. Such discussions make 'news'. Often they touch on matters which affect human well-being very deeply and so, understandably, the public at large are interested in the major moral questions they raise. By joining in the public debate moral theologians may perhaps be able to offer a Christian dimension to the common human concern to ensure that new technology enhances rather than diminishes humankind's possibilities for living truly human lives. Moreover, when they do this, they would seem to have the encouragement of Vatican II that they should feel free to present the truth as they see it:

> In order that such persons may fulfil their proper function, let it be recognized that all the faithful, clerical and lay, possess a lawful freedom of enquiry and of thought, and the freedom to express their minds humbly and courageously about those matters in which they enjoy competence. (*Gaudium et Spes*, n. 62)

In my paper to the consultation between bishops and moral theologians referred to earlier, I went on to say:

> If we are to be in tune with the spirit of our modern age, therefore, it is no longer possible to restrict moral theology to behind closed doors or to the privileged pages of some exclusive theological journal. Moral questions are the common fodder of open debate in the mass media. Moral theologians today are faced with a choice. Either they opt out of the dialogue: this might be a recipe for a quiet life removed from any tension with the hierarchical magisterium but it will be viewed by many moral theologians as a failure to be true to their ecclesial vocation. Or they decide to play their part in the dialogue. If they make this second option, they have no choice but to abide by the rules of dialogue. And Rule 1 is that they must be prepared to say what they honestly believe. Obviously, they can, and usually should, report the authentic teaching of the church, since that is part of the contribution they are expected to make. However, they must also be prepared to query that teaching whenever scientific discernment reveals that it is open to question. To be less than honest or to show a lack of scientific discernment *vis-à-vis* authentic

teaching is to surrender one's credibility in the dialogue. Moreover, such a stance harms the credibility of the church itself, if it is suspected that the reticence of moral theologians might be occasioned by fear of church authorities taking punitive action against them.

When moral theologians participate in public dialogue in this way, especially when their contribution involves questioning some aspects of official teaching in the light of scientific and historical analysis, understandably this becomes a further occasion for possible tension between them and the papal and episcopal magisterium. However, provided that moral theologians who question official teaching in such circumstances are (1) motivated by a real love and concern for the Church and its mission and also for the integrity of its teaching and (2) do not reject the competence of the hierarchical magisterium to issue authoritative teaching, then their contribution in the public dialogue should be interpreted as an attempt to help rather than oppose the papal and episcopal magisterium. These are two good indications that their questioning should not be interpreted as betraying an attitude 'of general opposition to church teaching' (n. 32). Good moral theology must not be equated with novel thinking. Yet neither must it be reduced to a mere repetition of past or present papal and episcopal teaching. As US Bishop Malone comments: 'Theologians without an appetite for creativity and development will not serve us well in an age where knowledge grows by quantum leaps' (in *Origins* (31 July 1986), p. 174).

Conclusion

I began this book by linking its theme with that of evangelization. I would like to end by suggesting that the involvement of moral theologians in public discussion of a whole host of ethical problems which are of urgent concern to our modern world should be given every encouragement. This should be the case even though on occasion a moral theologian might have to express his or her honest disagreement with some point of arguable teaching of the papal and episcopal magisterium. My reason for suggesting this is because I firmly believe that such participation by competent moral theologians in this kind of public dialogue is an important aspect of their sharing in the missionary activity of the Church according to their particular charism as moral theologians. Thesis 3, n. 4 of the International Theological Commission's document *The Magisterium and the Role of Theologians in the Church* brings this out when it says that both theologians and the magisterium 'are bound by the pastoral and missionary care they must have towards the world' and then proceeds to insist that 'the scientific character of the theologians' work does not free them from pastoral and missionary responsibility, especially in view of how quickly even scientific matters are given publicity by modern means of communication'. Otto Semmelroth, in his commentary on this thesis, stresses this missionary role of theology and agrees that it 'cannot be behind closed doors'. If, as *Gaudium et Spes* (n. 16) insists, Christians are conscience-bound to 'join with the rest of people in the search for truth, and for the genuine solution to the numerous problems which arise in the life of individuals and from social relationships', moral theologians would be failing in their 'ecclesial vocation' in the Church if they refused to participate in this common search by contributing to the dialogue according to their particular charism and competence.

INDEX